EVERYMAN'S LIBRARY
POCKET POETS

Garden Poems

Selected and edited by
John Hollander

EVERYMAN'S LIBRARY

POCKET POETS

Alfred A. Knopf · New York · Toronto

This selection by John Hollander first published in
Everyman's Library, 1996
Copyright © 1996 by David Campbell Publishers Ltd.
Second printing

A list of acknowledgments to copyright owners can be found at the back of
this volume.

ISBN 0-679-44726-1

Typography by Peter B. Willberg

Typeset in the UK by AccComputing, Castle Cary, Somerset

Printed and bound in Germany by
Graphischer Grossbetrieb Pössneck GmbH

CONTENTS

Foreword   13

PARADISES

JOHN MILTON Eden   19

OVID Before Gardens: The Golden Age   21

HOMER The Gardens of Alcinous   23

GEORGE HERBERT Paradise   25

SABA A King's Garden World   26

ALFRED, LORD TENNYSON An Arabian Night
     Garden   29

NICHOLAS GRIMALD The Garden   32

THOM GUNN The Garden of the Gods   34

ISAAC ROSENBERG The Garden of Joy   36

ANTHONY HECHT La Condition Botanique   38

DEBORA GREGER The Garden   44

GARDENS OF LOVE

GEOFFREY CHAUCER Love's Garden   47

THOMAS CAMPION Cherry Ripe   49

ANGELO POLIZIANO She Finds Herself in a Garden   50

EDMUND SPENSER In the Bower of Bliss   52
                  The Garden of Adonis   54

JOHN DONNE Twicknam Garden   56

DANTE GABRIEL ROSSETTI Silent Noon   58

WILLIAM BLAKE The Garden of Love   59

JAY MACPHERSON The Garden of the Sexes   60

HART CRANE Garden Abstract   61

ANON. The Seeds of Love   62

ALGERNON CHARLES SWINBURNE The Garden of
      Proserpine   65

ADRIENNE RICH Design in Living Colors   69

EDNA ST. VINCENT MILLAY The Hardy Garden   71

GARDENS OF THE MIND

JAMES MERRILL A Vision of the Garden   75

ANDREW MARVELL The Garden   76

JAMES SHIRLEY The Garden   79

JAY MACPHERSON A Garden Shut   81

OCTAVIO PAZ A Doomed Garden   83

JOHN KEATS A Garden-Dream   85

YVOR WINTERS Time and the Garden   87

WALTER DE LA MARE Myself   88

GEORGE MEREDITH The Garden of Epicurus   89

NICOLAS BOILEAU The Garden of Writing   90

JOHN POMFRET No Barren Leaves   92

GARDENS AND SEASONS

EDNA ST. VINCENT MILLAY Spring in the Garden ..   97

JAMES THOMSON Late Spring   98

WILLIAM MORRIS Thunder in the Garden   100

WALLACE STEVENS Banal Sojourn   103

ROBERT PENN WARREN The Garden   104

ROBERT BRIDGES The Garden in September 106
CHRISTINA ROSSETTI An October Garden 108
DINO CAMPANA Autumn Garden 109
WILLIAM DEAN HOWELLS November 110
V. SACKVILLE-WEST Frost 111
ROBERT FROST A Winter Eden 112
ALFRED, LORD TENNYSON Song 113
SAIGYŌ In Winter 114

FLOWERS

HAN YÜ Flowering Plums 117
HAFIZ The Lesson of the Flowers 118
RENÉ RAPIN Of Roses and Hyacinths 120
ERASMUS DARWIN The Poppy 121
ROBERT HERRICK To a Bed of Tulips 122
WILLIAM CARLOS WILLIAMS The Tulip Bed 123
V. SACKVILLE-WEST The Rose 124
ROBERT BROWNING The Flower's Name 127
J. D. McCLATCHY Weeds 130
JALĀL AL-DĪN RŪMĪ What the Flowers Said 131
ALFRED, LORD TENNYSON Come into the garden,
   Maud 133

GARDENERS

ROBERT GRAVES Gardener 139
MARK VAN DOREN Gardener 140
ROBERT LOUIS STEVENSON The Gardener 142

DONALD DAVIE Gardens no Emblems 143
WILLIAM SHAKESPEARE The Gardener's Lesson .. 144
ROBERT FROST A Girl's Garden 146
HUGO VON HOFMANNSTHAL The Emperor of China
    Speaks 149
EDWARD THOMAS Digging 151
MONA VAN DUYN The Gardener to His God 152
WALTER SAVAGE LANDOR The Gardener 154

THE WORK OF THE GARDEN

THEODORE ROETHKE Transplanting 157
THOMAS RANDOLPH On Grafting 158
ANDREW MARVELL The Mower Against Gardens 159
L. J. M. COLUMELLA Autumnal Work 161
WILLIAM COWPER On Pruning 163
V. SACKVILLE-WEST Pruning in March 164
WILLIAM COWPER The Work of Gardening 166

GARDENS OF THE WILD

JOSEPH WARTON The Wild 171
HORACE Conservation 172
JOHN DYER Prospects 173
WILLIAM MASON Against Formal Gardens 175
EDMUND WALLER The Garden of Bermuda 176
ALGERNON CHARLES SWINBURNE The Mill Garden 178
RALPH WALDO EMERSON In my garden 181

CITY GARDENS

MARTIAL De Hortis Julii Martialis 185
PAUL VERLAINE L'Allée 187
TRUMBULL STICKNEY An Athenian Garden 188
WILLIAM CARLOS WILLIAMS The Widow's Lament
     in Springtime 190
HOWARD MOSS The Roof Garden 192
MAY SWENSON The Garden at St. John's 194
JOHN HOLLANDER The Garden 196
ROSANNA WARREN Garden 197

PUBLIC GARDENS

OSCAR WILDE Le Jardin des Tuileries 203
TS'AO P'I Lotus Lake 204
MATTHEW ARNOLD Lines Written in Kensington
     Gardens 205
RICHARD WILBUR Caserta Garden 208
MARTHA HOLLANDER Central Park 210
RAINER MARIA RILKE *From* The Parks 211

RUINED GARDENS

ALFRED, LORD TENNYSON *From* In Memoriam 215
EDWIN ARLINGTON ROBINSON The Garden 217
ALGERNON CHARLES SWINBURNE A Forsaken
     Garden 218
HERMAN MELVILLE The Ravaged Villa 222
HAN-SHAN In an Abandoned Garden 223

9

JOHN CLARE To a Bower 224
ELIZABETH BARRETT BROWNING *From* The Deserted
     Garden 225
THOMAS HARDY The Garden Seat 228

A GARDEN OF GARDENS

W. S. MERVIN What is a garden 231
E. E. CUMMINGS This is the garden 232
GEORGE GASCOIGNE The World as Garden 233
THOMAS HARDY Domicilium 235
ALFRED, LORD TENNYSON Suburban Garden 237
D. H. LAWRENCE Trees in the Garden 238
WILLIAM MORRIS A Garden by the Sea 239
BORIS PASTERNAK The Weeping Garden 241
ALEXANDER POPE The Garden 242
ELIZABETH JENNINGS Her Garden 244
ŌSHIMA RYŌTA And then... 245

Acknowledgments 247
Index of Authors 250

10

For Eleanor Perenyi, with love and admiration

FOREWORD

Gardens in themselves are essentially poetic, works of art constructed in the language of nature. Reciprocally, poems were thought of in the past as flowers (posy and *poesy* being associated, and collections of poems called *anthologies* or flower-garlands) as if they were the product of carefully tended gardens, carefully weeded of the irrelevant growth of ordinary language. Marianne Moore's famous observation that poetry, to be genuine, must present "imaginary gardens with real toads in them" partially invokes this older tradition. Actual gardens preexist all our oldest poetic fictions about them. But the relations of imagined and real gardens are complex, and the changes in each throughout history produce subsequent adaptations of the other. Our idea of Paradise (a Greek word, derived from a Persian one for an enclosed pleasure-garden) comes from the biblical story of Eden, an enclosed and perfect world forever lost to humanity. Eden, with perpetual spring and fall eternally coexisting, delivered up its vegetation without urging from a recalcitrant earth. Human gardens, carved out of the rest of nature, require work, but modern gardening lies somewhere between the labor of farming for subsistence and the exercise of a craft, whether professional or amateur.

The primal western texts celebrating gardens are in Genesis and the Odyssey (later ages took these to be the prototypes of the formal Continental, and wilder-looking English gardens), and in the Song of Songs, whence the perennial metaphor of the female beloved's body as an enclosed garden. Medieval allegorical poetry abounded in cloister-like gardens with fountains in the middle of them, and design and description followed each other. The rise of cities and the growth of both public parks and private plots allowed poetry to deal both with actual gardening and the mythology of gardens, and to make new, informal meditative allegories of them.

Here are poems of actual and imagined gardens of many sorts, the fictive ones being as historically and culturally varied as the real ones—poems of small private gardens, large public ones, gardens in cities and wildernesses conceived of as somehow paradisal. They range from China and Japan to our own backyards: from Andrew Marvell's famous garden of contemplative retirement to Howard Moss and May Swenson contemplating bits of garden in New York City; and from Edmund Spenser's visions of true and false paradises to Mona Van Duyn's contemporary prayer against false horticulture.

I have occasionally retitled selections from longer poems (and consistently in the case of the passages from V. Sackville-West's fine georgic *The Garden.*) But this not being a scholarly edition, I have not indicated these added titles with brackets. And I feel I should acknowledge a debt to John Dixon Hunt, owed by all concerned with the history and literature of gardening.

JOHN HOLLANDER

INSCRIPTION IN A GARDEN

If any flower that here is grown,
    Or any herb, may ease your pain,
Take and accompt it as your own,
    But recompense the like again;
        For some and some is honest play,
        And so my wife taught me to say.

If here to walk you take delight,
    Why, come and welcome, when you will;
If I bid you sup here this night,
    Bid me another time, and still
        Think some and some is honest play,
        For so my wife taught me to say.

Thus if you sup or dine with me,
    If you walk here or sit at ease,
If you desire the thing you see,
    And have the same your mind to please,
        Think some and some is honest play,
        And so my wife taught me to say.

GEORGE GASCOIGNE

PARADISES

GENESIS 2: 8–10

And the Lord God planted a garden eastward in Eden; and there he put the man whom he had formed.

And out of the ground made the Lord God to grow every tree that is pleasant to the sight, and good for food; the tree of life also in the midst of the garden, and the tree of knowledge of good and evil.

And a river went out of Eden to water the garden; and from thence it was parted, and became into four heads.

KING JAMES BIBLE

EDEN

Southward through Eden went a river large,
Nor changed his course, but through the shaggy hill
Passed underneath engulfed, for God had thrown
That mountain as his garden mould, high raised
Upon the rapid current, which through veins
Of porous earth with kindly thirst up drawn,
Rose a fresh fountain, and with many a rill
Watered the garden; thence united fell
Down the steep glade, and met the nether flood,
Which from his darksome passage now appears,
And now divided into four main streams
Runs diverse, wandering many a famous realm
And country whereof here needs no account;
But rather to tell how, if art could tell,
How from that sapphire fount the crispèd brooks,
Rolling on orient pearl and sands of gold,
With mazy error under pendant shades
Ran nectar, visiting each plant, and fed
Flowers worthy of Paradise, which not nice art
In beds and curious knots, but Nature boon
Poured forth profuse on hill and dale and plain,
Both where the morning sun first warmly smote
The open field, and where the unpierced shade
Embrowned the noontide bowers. Thus was this place,
A happy rural seat of various view;

Groves whose rich trees wept odorous gums and balm,
Others whose fruit burnished with golden rind
Hung amiable, Hesperian fables true,
If true, here only, and of delicious taste.
Betwixt them lawns, or level downs, and flocks
Grazing the tender herb, were interposed,
Or palmy hillock, or the flowery lap
Of some irriguous valley spread her store,
Flowers of all hue, and without thorn the rose.
Another side, umbrageous grots and caves
Of cool recess, o'er which the mantling vine
Lays forth her purple grape, and gently creeps
Luxuriant; meanwhile murmuring waters fall
Down the slope hills, dispersed, or in a lake,
That to the fringèd bank with myrtle crowned
Her crystal mirror holds, unite their streams.
The birds their quire apply; airs, vernal airs,
Breathing the smell of field and grove, attune
The trembling leaves, while universal Pan,
Knit with the Graces and the Hours in dance,
Led on the eternal spring.

BEFORE GARDENS: THE GOLDEN AGE

Then sprang up first the golden age, which of itself
    maintained
The truth and right of everything, unforced and
    unconstrained.
There was no fear of punishment, there was no
    threatening law
In brazen tables nailèd up to keep the folk in awe.
There was no man would crouch or creep to Judge,
    with cap in hand:
They livèd safe without a Judge in every realm and land.
The lofty pine tree was not hewn from mountains
    where it stood,
In seeking strange and foreign lands, to rove upon the
    flood.
Men knew no other countries yet than where
    themselves did keep;
There was no town enclosèd yet, with walls and
    ditches deep.
No horn nor trumpet was in use, no sword or helmet
    worn:
The world was such that soldiers' help might easily be
    forborn.
The fertile earth as yet was free, untouched of spade or
    plough,
And yet it yielded of itself of every thing enough.

And men themselves, contented well with plain and
    simple food,
That on the earth of nature's gift, without their travail
    stood,
Did live by raspis, hips and haws, by cornels, plums
    and cherries,
By sloes and apples, nuts and pears, and loathsome
    bramble berries,
And by the acorns dropped on ground from Jove's
    broad tree in field.
The springtime lasted all the year, and Zephyr with his
    mild
And gentle blast did cherish things that grew of own
    accord,
The ground untilled, all kinds of fruit did plenteously
    afford.
No muck nor tillage was disposed on lean and barren
    land,
To make the crops of better head, and ranker for to
    stand.
Then streams ran milk, then streams ran wine, and
    yellow honey flowed
From each green tree whereon the rays of fiery
    Phœbus glowed.

TRANSLATED BY ARTHUR GOLDING

THE GARDENS OF ALCINOUS

Close to the gates a spacious garden lies,
From storms defended, and inclement skies:
Four acres was the allotted space of ground,
Fenced with a green enclosure all around.
Tall thriving trees confessed the fruitful mould;
The redening apple ripens here to gold,
Here the blue fig with luscious juice o'erflows,
With deeper red the full pomegranate glows,
Then branch here bends beneath the weighty pear,
And verdant olives flourish round the year.
The balmy spirit of the western gale
Eternal breathes on fruits untaught to fail;
Each dropping pear a following pear supplies,
On apples apples, figs on figs arise:
The same mild season gives the blooms to blow,
The buds to harden, and the fruits to grow.

  Here ordered vines in equal ranks appear
With all the united labours of the year;
Some to unload the fertile branches run,
Some dry the blackening clusters in the sun,
Others to tread the liquid harvest join,
The groaning presses foam with floods of wine.
Here are the vines in early flower descried,
Here grapes discoloured on the sunny side,
And there in autumn's richest purple dyed.

Beds of all various herbs, forever green,
In beauteous order terminate the scene.
    Two plenteous fountains the whole prospect
        crowned;
This through the gardens leads its streams around,
Visits each plant, and waters all the ground:
While that in pipes beneath the palace flows,
And thence its current on the town bestows;
To various use their various streams they bring,
The people one, and one supplies the King.

PARADISE

I bless thee, Lord, because I GROW
Among thy trees, which in a ROW
To thee both fruit and order OW.

What open force, or hidden CHARM
Can blast my fruit, or bring me HARM
While the inclosure is thine ARM?

Inclose me still for fear I START.
Be to me rather sharp and TART,
Than let me want thy hand and ART.

When thou dost greater judgements SPARE,
And with thy knife but prune and PARE,
Ev'n fruitful trees more fruitful ARE.

Such sharpness shows the sweetest FREND:
Such cuttings rather heal than REND:
And such beginnings touch their END.

A KING'S GARDEN WORLD

When the ruler decided to make flourishing the region
    of Rayy,
There were to be lofty castles to raise their summits to
    the castles of the sky.
The king established the plan of this garden of his kingdom,
So that the trees should be as green as the fortune of
    the king.
This garden Eram is comparable to the old garden Eram:

However, the ancient garden is grieved at comparing
    itself with the new,
In regard to those trees which have opened their green
    umbrellas to the Heavens,
And through which the sunshine makes a complicated
    pattern
Like the arrangement of the stars in the evening sky,
Or like the scattering of coins by the royal hand.
If a spray of the flowering bushes of this garden is not
    like Moses' bright hand,
Then why is its flowery aspect like the dawning of the
    stars,
And if the wind has not swept through the enclosure
    like the breath of Jesus,
Then why does the breath of its breezes bring life to
    the lifeless?

The famed Tuba tree is like a bramble bush beside
    these trees,
And the fountain of life like poison compared to its
    delicious waters.
The Tuba and the Sedra trees admire the trees of this
    garden;
Kasr and Tasmin envy the spray of these fountains.
If this garden is not Paradise, then why like Paradise,
Does it create happiness through its inner life?
Its enclosure is like the precincts of a drinking club,
And the young trees, like the imbibers, are full of gaiety;
And if the trees of this garden are not intoxicated, then
    why like drunkards
In conviviality do they embrace each others' necks?
A building is built by royal order in that garden
Whose glittering pinnacles make the sun seem dark;
Although the king of the seven regions has called it the
    "Eight Paradises,"
A name to be inscribed on the surface of Heaven,
Still its height is loftier than the seven heavens,
And its extent is greater than the original eight
    paradises.
No wonder then that when Mani and Azar saw its
    beautiful paintings,
They broke their brushes from shame.
Also in this garden was a flowing fountain like Tasmin
That has aroused the envy of the clear well of Zemzem.

The clear water of that pool is like the life-giving
    breath of Jesus,
And it seems that Mary may have washed her virgin-
    pure clothes in it.
This playing fountain, like the hand of the Shah,
Fills the earth and the sky with a shower of pearls.
I asked, "Is this the life-giving water?" and the answer
    came, "Yes."
I asked, "Is this garden Paradise?" and wisdom replied,
    "Certainly."
The king of kings called this garden Eram,
Although its namesake was not as wonderful as this
    new one.
When it was completed and its date was to be recorded,
All the poets took thought as to how it might be expressed;
Wisdom showed me the best solution and said, "Oh! Saba,
Tell the king of the world, the honour of nations,
That the breeze carried along the flowers through the
    garden Eram,"
And said for the date, "Let the garden Eram remain
    flourishing." . . .

AN ARABIAN NIGHT GARDEN

Above through many a bowery turn
A walk with vary-coloured shells
Wandered engrained. On either side
All round about the fragrant marge
From fluted vase, and brazen urn
In order, eastern flowers large,
Some dropping low their crimson bells
Half-closed, and others studded wide
 With disks and tiars, fed the time
 With odour in the golden prime
  Of good Haroun Alraschid.

Far off, and where the lemon grove
In closest coverture upsprung,
The living airs of middle night
Died round the bulbul as he sung;
Not he: but something which possessed
The darkness of the world, delight,
Life, anguish, death, immortal love,
Ceasing not, mingled, unrepressed,
 Apart from place, withholding time,
 But flattering the golden prime
  Of good Haroun Alraschid.

Black the garden-bowers and grots
Slumbered: the solemn palms were ranged
Above, unwooed of summer wind:
A sudden splendour from behind
Flushed all the leaves with rich gold-green,
And, flowing rapidly between
Their interspaces, counterchanged
The level lake with diamond-plots
   Of dark and bright. A lovely time,
    For it was in the golden prime
      Of good Haroun Alraschid.

Dark-blue the deep sphere overhead,
Distinct with vivid stars inlaid,
Grew darker from that under-flame:
So, leaping lightly from the boat,
With silver anchor left afloat,
In marvel whence that glory came
Upon me, as in sleep I sank
In cool soft turf upon the bank,
   Entrancèd with that place and time,
    So worthy of the golden prime
      Of good Haroun Alraschid.

Thence through the garden I was drawn –
A realm of pleasance, many a mound,
And many a shadow-chequered lawn
Full of the city's stilly sound,
And deep myrrh-thickets blowing round
The stately cedar, tamarisks,
Thick rosaries of scented thorn,
Tall orient shrubs, and obelisks
    Graven with emblems of the time,
    In honour of the golden prime
      Of good Haroun Alraschid ...

THE GARDEN

The issue of great Jove, draw near you Muses nine:
Help us to praise the blissful plot of garden ground so
    fine.
The garden gives good food, and aid for leeches' cure:
The garden, full of great delight, his master doth allure.
Sweet salad herbs be here, and herbs of every kind:
The ruddy grapes, the seemly fruits, be here at hand to
    find.
Here pleasance wanteth not, to make a man full fain:
Here marvellous the mixture is of solace and of gain.
To water sundry seeds, the furrow by the way
A running river, trilling down with liquor, can convey.
Behold, with lively hue fair flowers that shine so bright:
With riches, like the orient gems, they paint the mould
    in sight.
Bees, humming with soft sound (their murmur is so
    small),
Of blooms and blossoms suck the tops, on dewèd leaves
    they fall.
The creeping vine holds down her own bewedded elms,
And, wandering out with branches thick, reeds folded
    overwhelms.
Trees spread their coverts wide with shadows fresh
    and gay:

Full well their branchèd boughs defend the fervent sun
    away.
    Birds chatter, and some chirp, and some sweet tunes
      do yield:
All mirthful, with their songs so blithe, they make both
    air and field.
    The garden, it allures; it feeds, it glads the sprite:
From heavy hearts all doleful dumps the garden
    chaseth quite.
    Strength it restores to limbs, draws and fulfills the
      sight,
With cheer revives the senses all, and maketh labour
    light.
    O, what delights to us the garden ground doth bring?
Seed, leaf, flower, fruit, herb, bee, and tree, and more,
    then I may sing.

THE GARDEN OF THE GODS

All plants grow here; the most minute,
　　Glowing from turf, is in its place.
　　The constant vision of the race:
Lawned orchard deep with flower and fruit.

So bright, that some who see it near,
　　Think there is lapis on the stems,
　　And think green, blue, and crimson gems
Hang from the vines and briars here.

They follow path to path in wonder
　　Through the intense undazzling light.
　　Nowhere does blossom flare so white!
Nowhere so black is earthmould under!

It goes, though it may come again.
　　But if at last they try to tell,
　　They search for trope or parallel,
And cannot, after all, explain.

It was sufficient, there, to be,
　　And meaning, thus, was superseded.
　　– Night circles it, it has receded,
Distant and difficult to see.

Where my foot rests, I hear the creak
   From generations of my kin,
   Layer on layer, pressed leaf-thin.
They merely are. They cannot speak.

This was the garden's place of birth:
   I trace it downward from my mind,
   Through breast and calf I feel it vined,
And rooted in the death-rich earth.

THE GARDEN OF JOY

In honey essenced bliss of sleep's deceit
My sense lay drowned, and my soul's eyes saw clear,
Unstranged to wonder, made familiar
By instant seeing. Eden's garden sweet,
Shedding upon mine eyelids odorous heat
Of the light fingered golden atmosphere
Shaken through boughs whose whispering I could hear.
Beneath, within the covert's cool retreat
Of the spread boughs stood shapes who swayed the
        boughs,
And bright fruit fell, laughing to leave green house;
While gleeful children dabbled with the sun
Caught the strange fruit, then ran with smiles of love
To earth, whose peoples as they ate thereof
Soft sank into the garden, one by one.

They lie within the garden, outside Time.
The ripened fulness of their soul's desire
Glad on their tranquil faces. No fanged fire
Of hot insatiate pleasure, no pulsed chime
To summon to tusked orgy of earth's slime,
Flickers the throne of rapture's flushed empire
That glows, mild rays of the divine attire
Upon each face, sun of this day-spring clime.

They seem forever wondering – listening
Unto some tale of marvel, music told,
That the flowers weep in jewelled glistening
With envy of the joy that they must hold,
While in the dewy mirrors lady Spring
Trims herself by their smiles, their happy mould.

LA CONDITION BOTANIQUE

    Romans, rheumatic, gouty, came
  To bathe in Ischian springs where water steamed,
Puffed and enlarged their bold imperial thoughts, and
    which
Later Madame Curie declared to be so rich
  In radioactive content as she deemed
    Should win them everlasting fame.

    Scattered throughout their ice and snow
  The Finns have built airtight cabins of log
Where they may lie, limp and entranced by the
    sedative purr
Of steam pipes, or torment themselves with flails of fir
  To stimulate the blood, and swill down grog,
    Setting the particles aglow.

    Similarly the Turks, but know
  Nothing of the more delicate thin sweat
Of plants, breathing their scented oxygen upon
Brooklyn's botanical gardens, roofed with glass and run
  So to the pleasure of each leafy pet,
    Manured, addressed in Latin, so

To its thermostatic happiness –
Spreading its green and innocence to the ground
Where pipes, like Satan masquerading as the snake,
Coil and uncoil their frightful liquid length, and make
Gurglings of love mixed with a rumbling sound
Of sharp intestinal distress –

So to its pleasure, as I said,
That each particular vegetable may thrive,
Early and late, as in the lot first given Man,
Sans interruption, as when Universal Pan
Led on the Eternal Spring. The spears of chive,
The sensitive plant, showing its dread,

The Mexican flytrap, that can knit
Its quilled jaws pitilessly, and would hurt
A fly with pleasure, leading Riley's life in bed
Of peat moss and of chemicals, and is thoughtfully fed
Flies for the entrée, flies for the dessert,
Fruit flies for fruit, and all of it

Administered as by a wife –
Lilith our lady, patroness of plants,
Who sings, *Lullay myn lykyng, myn owyn dere derlyng,*
Madrigals nightly to the spiny stalk in sterling
Whole notes of admiration and romance –
This, then is what is called The Life.

And we, like disinherited heirs,
  Old Adams, can inspect the void estate
At visiting hours: the unconditional garden spot,
The effortless innocence preserved, for God knows what,
  And think, as we depart by the toll gate:
    No one has lived here these five thousand years.

  Our world is turned on points, is whirled
  On wheels, Tibetan prayer wheels, French verb wheels,
The toothy wheels of progress, the terrible torque
Insisting, and in the sky, even above New York
  Rotate the marvelous four-fangled seals
    Ezekiel saw. The mother-of-pearled

  Home of the bachelor oyster lies
  Fondled in fluent shifts of bile and lime
As sunlight strikes the water, and it is of our world,
And will appear to us sometime where the finger is curled
  Between the frets upon a mandolin,
    Fancy cigar boxes, and eyes

  Of ceremonial masks; and all
  The places where Kilroy inscribed his name,
For instance, the ladies' rest room in the Gare du Nord,
The iron rump of Buddha, whose hallowed, hollowed core
  Admitted tourists once but all the same
    Housed a machine gun, and let fall

A killing fire from its eyes
During the war; and Polyphemus hurled
Tremendous rocks that stand today off Sicily's coast
Signed with the famous scrawl of our most traveled ghost;
And all these various things are of our world.
But what's become of Paradise?

Ah, it is lodged in glass, survives
In Brooklyn, like a throwback, out of style,
Like an incomprehensible veteran of the Grand
Army of the Republic in the reviewing stand
Who sees young men in a mud-colored file
March to the summit of their lives,

For glory, for their country, with the flag
Joining divergent stars of North and South
In one blue field of heaven, till they fall in blood
And are returned at last unto their native mud –
The eyes weighed down with stones, the sometimes
mouth
Helpless to masticate or gag

Its old inheritance of earth.
    In the sweat of thy face shalt thou manage,
            said the Lord.
And we, old Adams, stare through the glass panes
            and wince,
Fearing to see the ancestral apple, pear, or quince,
    The delicacy of knowledge, the fleshed Word,
        The globe of wisdom that was worth

        Our lives, or so our parents thought,
    And turn away to strengthen our poor breath
And body, keep the flesh rosy with hopeful dreams,
Peach-colored, practical, to decorate the bones,
            with schemes
    Of life insurance, Ice-Cream-After-Death,
        Hormone injections, against the *mort'*

        Saison, largely to babble praise
    Of Simeon Pyrites, patron saint
Of our Fools' Paradise, whose glittering effigy
Shines in God's normal sunlight till the blind men see
    Visions as permanent as artists paint:
        The body's firm, nothing decays

Upon the heirloom set of bones
In their gavotte. Yet we look through the glass
Where green lies ageless under snow-stacked roofs
    in steam-
Fitted apartments, and reflect how bud and stem
  Are wholly flesh, and the immaculate grass
    Does without buttressing of bones.

In open field or public bed
  With ultraviolet help, man hopes to learn
The leafy secret, pay his most outstanding debt
To God in the salt and honesty of his sweat,
  And in his streaming face manly to earn
    His daily and all-nourishing bread.

THE GARDEN

The ducks have turned to stone, the lovers untwined
    and straggled to their separate beds.
Blossom upon lush blossom closes in on itself,

    the gardener closing the Carnivorous House,
the Venus flytrap close-lipped over a last luckless fly.
    Night-blooming cereus opens

to a world ever more shadowed, more dimly seen.
    Go back calls a thrush from the bramble hedge.
Think of that first garden after the gates were closed,

    paradise retaken by weeds once damned.
Around the poisonous buttercup, cows have chewed
    and now lie, stately, in a patch of shade.

In place of tears, the corners of their unblinking eyes
    are crawling with flies.
And there is evening and there is morning,
    an eighth day.

GARDENS OF LOVE

SONG OF SOLOMON 4: 12–16

A garden inclosed is my sister, my spouse; a spring shut up, a fountain sealed.

Thy plants are an orchard of pomegranates, with pleasant fruits; camphire, with spikenard,

Spikenard and saffron; calamus and cinnamon, with all trees of frankincense: myrrh and aloes, with all the chief spices:

A fountain of gardens, a well of living waters, and streams from Lebanon.

Awake, O north wind; and come, thou south; blow upon my garden, that the spices thereof may flow out. Let my beloved come into his garden, and eat his pleasant fruits.

KING JAMES BIBLE

LOVE'S GARDEN

A garden saw I full of blosmy boughs
Upon a river, in a grene mead,
There as sweetness evermore enow is,
With flowers white, blue, yellow, and red,
And colde welle-streames, nothing dead,
That swimmen full of smale fishes light,
With finnes red, and scales silver bright.

On every bough the briddes heard I sing
With voice of angel in their harmony;
Some busied them their briddes forth to bring;
The little conies to their play gone hie,
And further all about I gan espy
The dredful roe, the buck, the hart, the hind,
Squirrels, and beastes small of gentle kind.

Of instruments of stringes in accord
Heard I so play a ravishing sweetness
That God, that maker is of all and lord,
Ne hearde never better, as I guess.
Therewith a wind, unnethe it might be less,
Made in the leaves green a noise soft
Accordant to the fowles song aloft.

Th'air of that place so attempre was
That never was grievance of hot nor cold;
There wax eke every wholesome spice and grass:
No man may there waxe sick nor old.
Yet was there joye more a thousandfold
Than man can tell; nor never would it night,
But aye clear day to any mannes sight.

Under a tree, beside a well, I sey
Cupid, our lord, his arrows forge and file;
And at his feet his bow all ready lay,
And Will, his daughter, tempered all this while
The hevedes in the well, and with her will
She couched them, after they should serve,
Some for to slay, and some to wound and carve.

CHERRY RIPE

There is a Garden in her face,
Where Roses and white Lillies grow;
   A heav'nly paradise is that place,
Wherein all pleasant fruits doe flow.
   There Cherries grow, which none may buy
   Till "Cherry ripe" themselves do cry.

Those Cherries fayrely doe enclose
Of Orient Pearle a double row;
   Which when her lovely laughter showes,
They look like Rose-buds fill'd with snow.
   Yet them nor Peer nor Prince can buy,
   Till "Cherry ripe" themselves do cry.

Her Eyes like Angels watch them still;
Her Browes like bended bowes do stand,
   Threatning with piercing frowns to kill
All that attempt with eye or hand
   Those sacred Cherries to come nigh,
   Till "Cherry ripe" themselves do cry.

SHE FINDS HERSELF IN A GARDEN

I found myself, girls, early one fine day
All in a garden green and in mid-May;
In the green grass around me lilies blew
And violets, and other lovely new
Flowers: I reached to pluck and place them where
They'd make a wreath adorning my blonde hair
And crown the locks of my belovèd, too.
I found myself, girls . . .

But when my skirt was full of flowers, I
Saw many roses – of no single hue –
And ran to them to heap my whole lap high
They smelled so lovely, having shed the dew,
With sweet desire and divine delight
My heart awakened, and was stirred anew.
I found myself, girls . . .

I thought that I could never let you know
How lovely all those roses were – some few
Had, bursting from their buds, commenced to blow,
Some had begun to blast, some were quite new;
And the Love told me "Go and gather those
Which on the thorn there bloom most fair and true".
I found myself, girls . . .

When every petal's opened up, and when
It is most beautiful and welcome too,
Then is the rose for weaving into wreaths;
Before its beauty has quite fled, let's then
Gather, girls, the while its youth still breathes
The fairest rose that ever in garden grew.
I found myself, girls . . .

ANGELO POLIZIANO

TRANSLATED BY JOHN HOLLANDER

IN THE BOWER OF BLISS

There the most daintie paradise on ground
It selfe doth offer to his sober eye,
In which all pleasures plenteously abownd,
And none does others happinesse envye:
The painted flowres, the trees upshooting hye,
The dales for shade, the hilles for breathing space,
The trembling groves, the christall running by;
And that which all faire workes doth most aggrace,
The art, which all that wrought, appeared in no place.

One would have thought, (so cunningly the rude
And scorned partes were mingled with the fine,)
That Nature had for wantonesse ensude
Art, and that Art at Nature did repine;
So striving each th' other to undermine,
Each did the others work more beautify;
So diff'ring both in willes agreed in fine:
So all agreed through sweete diversity,
This gardin to adorne with all variety.

And in the midst of all a fountaine stood,
Of richest substance that on earth might bee,
So pure and shiny that the silver flood
Through every channell running one might see:
Most goodly it with curious ymageree

Was overwrought, and shapes of naked boyes,
Of which some seemd with lively jollitee
To fly about playing their wanton toyes,
Whylest others did them selves embay in liquid joyes.

And over all, of purest gold was spred
A trayle of yvie in his native hew:
For the rich metall was so coloured,
That wight, who did not well avis'd it vew,
Would surely deeme it to bee yvie trew:
Low his lascivious armes adown did creepe,
That themselves dipping in the silver dew,
Their fleecy flowres they tenderly did steepe,
Which drops of christall seemd for wantones to weep.

Infinit streames continually did well
Out of this fountaine, sweet and faire to see,
The which into an ample laver fell,
And shortly grew to so great quantitie,
That like a litle lake it seemd to bee;
Whose depth exceeded not three cubits hight,
That through the waves one might the bottom see,
All pav'd beneath with jaspar shining bright,
That seemd the fountaine in that sea did sayle upright.

THE GARDEN OF ADONIS

There is continuall spring, and harvest there
Continuall, both meeting at one tyme:
For both the boughes doe laughing blossoms beare,
And with fresh colours decke the wanton pryme,
And eke attonce the heavy trees they clyme,
Which seeme to labour under their fruites lode:
The whiles the joyous birdes make their pastyme
Emongst the shady leaves, their sweet abode,
And their trew loves without suspition tell abrode.

Right in the middest of that paradise
There stood a stately mount, on whose round top
A gloomy grove of mirtle trees did rise,
Whose shady boughes sharp steele did never lop,
Nor wicked beastes their tender buds did crop,
But like a girlond compassed the hight,
And from their fruitfull sydes sweet gum did drop,
That all the ground, with pretious deaw bedight,
Threw forth most dainty odours, and most sweet delight.

And in the thickest covert of that shade
There was a pleasaunt arber, not by art,
But of the trees owne inclination made,
Which knitting their rancke braunches part to part,
With wanton yvie twyne entrayld athwart,

And eglantine and caprifole emong,
Fashiond above within their inmost part,
That nether Phœbus beams could through them throng,
Nor Aeolus sharp blast could worke them any wrong.

And all about grew every sort of flowre,
To which sad lovers were transformde of yore;
Fresh Hyacinthus, Phœbus paramoure
And dearest love,
Foolish Narcisse, that likes the watry shore,
Sad Amaranthus, made a flowre but late,
Sad Amaranthus, in whose purple gore
Me seemes I see Amintas wretched fate,
To whom sweet poets verse hath given endlesse date.

There wont fayre Venus often to enjoy
Her deare Adonis joyous company,
And reape sweet pleasure of the wanton boy:
There yet, some say, in secret he does ly,
Lapped in flowres and pretious spycery,
By her hid from the world, and from the skill
Of Stygian gods, which doe her love envy;
But she her selfe, when ever that she will,
Possesseth him, and of his sweetnesse takes her fill.

TWICKNAM GARDEN

Blasted with sighs, and surrounded with tears,
    Hither I come to seek the spring,
    And at mine eyes, and at mine ears,
Receive such balms, as else cure everything;
    But O, self traitor, I do bring
The spider love, which transubstantiates all,
    And can convert manna to gall,
And that this place may thoroughly be thought
    True paradise, I have the serpent brought.

'Twere wholesomer for me, that winter did
    Benight the glory of this place,
    And that a grave frost did forbid
These trees to laugh, and mock me to my face;
    But that I may not this disgrace
Endure, nor yet leave loving, Love, let me
    Some senseless piece of this place be;
Make me a mandrake, so I may groan here,
    Or a stone fountain weeping out my year.

Hither with crystal vials, lovers come,
    And take my tears, which are love's wine,
    And try your mistress' tears at home,
For all are false, that taste not just like mine;
    Alas, hearts do not in eyes shine,
Not can you more judge woman's thoughts by tears,
    Than by her shadow, what she wears.
O perverse sex, where none is true but she,
    Who's therefore true, because her truth kills me.

SILENT NOON

Your hands lie open in the long fresh grass, —
    The finger-points look through like rosy blooms:
    Your eyes smile peace. The pasture gleams and glooms
'Neath billowing skies that scatter and amass.
All round our nest, far as the eye can pass,
    Are golden kingcup-fields with silver edge
    Where the cow-parsley skirts the hawthorn-hedge.
'Tis visible silence, still as the hour-glass.

Deep in the sun-searched growths the dragon-fly
Hangs like a blue thread loosened from the sky: —
    So this wing'd hour is dropt to us from above.
Oh! clasp we to our hearts, for deathless dower,
This close-companioned inarticulate hour
    When twofold silence was the song of love.

THE GARDEN OF LOVE

I went to the Garden of Love
And saw what I never had seen:
A Chapel was built in the midst,
Where I used to play on the green.

And the gates of this Chapel were shut,
And Thou shalt not. writ over the door;
So I turn'd to the Garden of Love,
That so many sweet flowers bore.

And I saw it was filled with graves,
And tomb-stones where flowers should be:
And Priests in black gowns, were walking their rounds,
And binding with briars, my joys & desires.

THE GARDEN OF THE SEXES

I have a garden closed away
And shadowed from the light of day
Where Love hangs bound on every tree
And I alone go free.

His sighs, that turn the weathers round,
His tears, that water all the ground,
His blood, that reddens in the vine,
These all are mine.

At night the golden apple-tree
Is my fixed station, whence I see
Terrible, sublime and free,
My loves go wheeling over me.

GARDEN ABSTRACT

The apple on its bough is her desire, –
Shining suspension, mimic of the sun.
The bough has caught her breath up, and her voice,
Dumbly articulate in the slant and rise
Of branch on branch above her, blurs her eyes.
She is prisoner of the tree and its green fingers.

And so she comes to dream herself the tree,
The wind possessing her, weaving her young veins,
Holding her to the sky and its quick blue,
Drowning the fever of her hands in sunlight.
She has no memory, nor fear, nor hope
Beyond the grass and shadows at her feet.

THE SEEDS OF LOVE

I sowed the seeds of love,
'Twas early in the Spring,
In April and May, and in June likewise,
The small birds they do sing.

My garden is well planted
With flowers everywhere,
But I had not the liberty to choose for myself
Of the flowers that I loved dear.

My gardener he stood by,
I asked him to choose for me;
He chose me the violet, the lily and the pink,
But these I refused all three.

The violet I forsook
Because it fades so soon.
The lily and the pink I did overlook
And vowed I'd stay till June.

For in June there's a red rosebud,
And that's the flower for me,
So I pulled and I plucked at the red rosebud
Till I gained the willow tree.

For the willow tree will twist
And the willow tree will twine,
I wish I was in a young man's arms
That once had this heart of mine.

My gardener he stood by,
And he told me to take good care;
For in the middle of the red rosebud
There grew a sharp thorn there.

I told him I'd take no care
Until I felt the smart.
I pulled and I plucked at the red rosebud
Till it pierced me to my heart.

I lockèd up my garden gate,
Resolving to keep the key,
But a young man came a-courting me
And he stole my heart away.

My garden is over-run
No flowers in it grew,
For the beds that was once covered with sweet thyme
They are now over-run with rue.

Come all you false young men
That leave me here to complain
For the grass that is now trodden under foot
In time it will rise again.

64   ANON.

COLLECTED BY CECIL SHARP

THE GARDEN OF PROSERPINE

Here, where the world is quiet,
   Here, where all trouble seems
Dead winds' and spent waves' riot
   In doubtful dreams of dreams;
I watch the green field growing
For reaping folk and sowing,
For harvest time and mowing,
   A sleepy world of streams.

I am tired of tears and laughter,
   And men that laugh and weep,
Of what may come hereafter
   For men that sow to reap:
I am weary of days and hours,
Blown buds of barren flowers,
Desires and dreams and powers
   And everything but sleep.

Here life has death for neighbour,
   And far from eye or ear
Wan waves and wet winds labour,
   Weak ships and spirits steer;
They drive adrift, and whither
They wot not who make thither;
But no such winds blow hither,
   And no such things grow here.

No growth of moor or coppice,
　　No heather-flower or vine,
But bloomless buds of poppies,
　　Green grapes of Proserpine,
Pale beds of blowing rushes
Where no leaf blooms or blushes,
Save this whereout she crushes
　　For dead men deadly wine.

Pale, without name or number,
　　In fruitless fields of corn,
They bow themselves and slumber
　　All night till light is born;
And like a soul belated,
In hell and heaven unmated,
By cloud and mist abated
　　Comes out of darkness morn.

Though one were strong as seven,
　　He too with death shall dwell,
Nor wake with wings in heaven,
　　Nor weep for pains in hell;
Though one were fair as roses,
His beauty clouds and closes;
And well though love reposes,
　　In the end it is not well.

Pale, beyond porch and portal,
    Crowned with calm leaves, she stands
Who gathers all things mortal
    With cold immortal hands;
Her languid lips are sweeter
Than love's who fears to greet her
To men that mix and meet her
    From many times and lands.

She waits for each and other,
    She waits for all men born;
Forgets the earth her mother,
    The life of fruits and corn;
And spring and seed and swallow
Take wing for her and follow
Where summer song rings hollow
    And flowers are put to scorn.

There go the loves that wither,
    The old loves with wearier wings;
And all dead years draw thither,
    And all disastrous things;
Dead dreams of days forsaken
Blind buds that snows have shaken,
Wild leaves that winds have taken,
    Red strays of ruined springs.

We are not sure of sorrow,
    And joy was never sure;
To–day will die to–morrow;
    Time stoops to no man's lure;
And love, grown faint and fretful
With lips but half regretful
Sighs, and with eyes forgetful
    Weeps that no loves endure.

From too much love of living,
    From hope and fear set free,
We thank with brief thanksgiving
    Whatever gods may be
That no life lives for ever;
That dead men rise up never;
That even the weariest river
    Winds somewhere safe to sea.

Then star nor sun shall waken,
    Nor any change of light:
Nor sound of waters shaken
    Nor any sound or sight:
Nor wintry leaves nor vernal,
Nor days nor things diurnal;
Only the sleep eternal
    In an eternal night.

DESIGN IN LIVING COLORS

Embroidered in a tapestry of green
Among the textures of a threaded garden,
The gesturing lady and her paladin
Walk in a path where shade and sunlight harden
Upon the formal attitudes of trees
By no wind bent, and birds without a tune,
Against the background of a figured frieze
In an eternal summer afternoon.

So you and I in our accepted frame
Believe a casual world of bricks and flowers
And scarcely guess what symbols wander tame
Among the panels of familiar hours.
Yet should the parting boughs of green reveal
A slender unicorn with jeweled feet,
Could I persuade him at my touch to kneel
And from my fingers take what unicorns eat?

If you should pick me at my whim a rose,
Setting the birds upon the bush in flight,
How should I know what crimson meaning grows
Deep in this garden, where such birds alight?
And how should I believe, the meaning clear,
That we are children of disordered days?
That fragmentary world is mended here,
And in this air a clearer sunlight plays.

The fleeing hare, the wings that brush the tree,
All images once separate and alone,
Become the creatures of a tapestry
Miraculously stirred and made our own.
We are the denizens of a living wood
Where insight blooms anew on every bough,
And every flower emerges understood
Out of a pattern unperceived till now.

THE HARDY GARDEN

Now let forever the phlox and the rose be tended
Here where the rain has darkened and the sun has dried
So many times the terrace, yet is love unended,
    Love has not died.

Let here no seed of a season, that the winter
But once assails, take root and for a time endure;
But only such as harbour at the frozen centre
    The germ secure.

Set here the phlox and the iris, and establish
Pink and valerian, and the great and lesser bells;
But suffer not the sisters of the year, to publish
    That frost prevails.

How far from home in a world of mortal burdens
Is Love, that may not die, and is forever young!
Set roses here: surround her only with such maidens
    As speak her tongue.

GARDENS OF THE MIND

All who are sick at heart and cry in bitterness,
Let not your soul complain in grief.
Enter the garden of my songs, and find balm
For your sorrow, and sing there with open-mouth.
Honey compared with them is bitter to the taste,
And before their scent, flowing myrrh is rank.
Through them the deaf hear, the stutterers speak,
The blind see, and the halting run.
The troubled and grief-stricken rejoice in them,
All who are sick at heart, and cry in bitterness.

MOSES IBN EZRA
TRANSLATED BY DAVID GOLDSTEIN
"THE GARDEN OF SONG"

A VISION OF THE GARDEN

One winter morning as a child
Upon the windowpane's thin frost I drew
Forehead and eyes and mouth the clear and mild
Features of nobody I knew

And then abstracted looking through
This or that wet transparent line
Beyond beheld a winter garden so
Heavy with snow its hedge of pine

And sun so brilliant on the snow
I breathed my pleasure out onto the chill pane
Only to see its angel fade in mist.
I was a child, I did not know

That what I longed for would resist
Neither what cold lines should my finger trace
On colder grounds before I found anew
In yours the features of that face

Whose words whose looks alone undo
Such frosts I lay me down in love in fear
At how they melt become a blossoming pear
Joy outstretched in our bodies' place.

THE GARDEN

How vainly men themselves amaze
To win the palm, the oak, or bays,
And their incessant labours see
Crowned from some single herb, or tree,
Whose short and narrow-vergèd shade
Does prudently their toils upbraid;
While all flowers and all trees do close
To weave the garlands of repose!

Fair Quiet, have I found thee here,
And Innocence, thy sister dear?
Mistaken long, I sought you then
In busy companies of men.
Your sacred plants, if here below,
Only among the plants will grow;
Society is all but rude
To this delicious solitude.

No white nor red was ever seen
So amorous as this lovely green.
Fond lovers, cruel as their flame,
Cut in these trees their mistress' name:
Little, alas, they know or heed
How far these beauties hers exceed!
Fair trees, wheresoe'er your barks I wound,
No name shall but your own be found.

When we have run our passion's heat,
Love hither makes his best retreat.
The gods, that mortal beauty chase,
Still in a tree did end their race:
Apollo hunted Daphne so,
Only that she might laurel grow;
And Pan did after Syrinx speed,
Not as a nymph, but for a reed.

What wondrous life is this I lead!
Ripe apples drop about my head;
The luscious clusters of the vine
Upon my mouth do crush their wine;
The nectarine and curious peach
Into my hands themselves do reach;
Stumbling on melons, as I pass,
Ensnared with flowers, I fall on grass.

Meanwhile the mind from pleasure less
Withdraws into its happiness;
The mind, that ocean where each kind
Does straight its own resemblance find;
Yet it creates, transcending these,
Far other worlds and other seas,
Annihilating all that's made
To a green thought in a green shade.

Here at the fountain's sliding foot,
Or at some fruit-tree's mossy root,
Casting the body's vest aside,
My soul into the boughs does glide:
There, like a bird, it sits and sings,
Then whets and combs its silver wings,
And, till prepared for longer flight,
Waves in its plumes the various light.

Such was that happy garden-state,
While man there walked without a mate:
After a place so pure and sweet,
What other help could yet be meet!
But 'twas beyond a mortal's share
To wander solitary there:
Two paradises 'twere in one
To live in Paradise alone.

How well the skilful gardener drew,
Of flowers and herbs, this dial new;
Where, from above, the milder sun
Does through a fragrant zodiac run;
And, as it works, the industrious bee
Computes its time as well as we!
How could such sweet and wholesome hours
Be reckoned but with herbs and flowers?

THE GARDEN

This garden does not take my eyes,
Though here you show how art of men
Can purchase nature at a price
Would stock old paradise again.

These glories while you dote upon,
I envy not your spring nor pride,
Nay boast the summer all your own,
My thoughts with less are satisfied.

Give me a little plot of ground,
Where might I with the sun agree,
Though every day he walk the round,
My garden he should seldom see.

Those tulips that such wealth display,
To court my eye, shall lose their name,
Though now they listen, as if they
Expected I should praise their flame.

But I would see my self appear
Within the violet's drooping head,
On which a melancholy tear
The discontented morn hath shed.

Within their buds let roses sleep,
And virgin lilies on their stem,
Till sighs from lovers glide, and creep
Into their leaves to open them.

I'the centre of my ground compose
Of bays and yew my summer room,
Which may so oft as I repose,
Present my arbour, and my tomb.

No woman here shall find me out,
Or if a chance do bring one hither,
I'll be secure, for round about
I'll moat it with my eyes' foul weather.

No bird shall live within my pale,
To charm me with their shames of art,
Unless some wandering nightingale
Come here to sing, and break her heart.

Upon whose death I'll try to write
An epitaph in some funeral stone,
So sad, and true, it may invite
My self to die, and prove my own.

A GARDEN SHUT

A garden shut, a fountain sealed,
And all the shadowed mountains yield:
Dear Reader sits among the rocks
And fiddles at my seven locks.

How green my little world is grown
To entertain the man of stone!
The green man in the garden's lap
Draws his fill of vital sap,
But when the south wind blows is seen
Spineless as any other green.
The stone man with his burden on
Stands as stiff as Solomon,
Or wintry Herod made his heir –
Small comfort for my garden there.

The fishes in my garden's eye
Like thoughts, or thoughts like fish go by.
The crystal of the morning air
Leads up the daughters mild and fair
Closed in their bells of tinkling glass
Precious as ever Sheba was,
To gently promenade the place,
This circle of their earthly race;
Till from the shade in pride and scorn

Bursts the impetuous Unicorn,
Shatters the day and blacks the sun,
Spits rudely on his sexual thorn
The virgins one by shrieking one,
Crushes the green, and fells the stone,
Breaks fountain, wall, and so is gone.

Reader, here is no place for you.
Go wander as the wild birds do,
And never once, in peace reposed,
Wonder on whom my garden closed.

A DOOMED GARDEN

A garden is not a place.
Down a path of reddish sand,
we enter a drop of water,
drink green clarities from its center,
we climb
        the spiral of hours
to the tip of the day,
                    descend
to the last burning of its ember.
Mumbling river,
                the garden flows through the night.

That one in Mixcoac, abandoned,
covered with scars,
                    was a body
at the point of collapse.
                    I was a boy,
and the garden for me was like a grandfather.
I clambered up its leafy knees,
not knowing it was doomed.
The garden knew it:
                    it awaited its destruction
as a condemned man awaits the axe.
The fig tree was a goddess,
                    the Mother.

Hum of irascible insects,
the muffled drums of the blood,
the sun and its hammer,
the green hug of innumerable limbs.
The cleft in the trunk:
                        the world half-opened.

I thought I had seen death:
                        I saw
the other face of being,
                        the feminine void,
the fixed featureless splendor.

❧

    TRANSLATED BY ELIOT WEINBERGER

A GARDEN-DREAM

Methought I stood where trees of every clime,
Palm, myrtle, oak, and sycamore, and beech,
With plantain, and spice-blossoms, made a screen;
In neighbourhood of fountains (by the noise
Soft-showering in my ears), and (by the touch
Of scent) not far from roses. Turning round
I saw an arbour with a drooping roof
Of trellis vines, and bells, and larger blooms,
Like floral censers, swinging light in air;
Before its wreathèd doorway, on a mound
Of moss, was spread a feast of summer fruits,
Which, nearer seen, seemed refuse of a meal
By angel tasted or our Mother Eve;
For empty shells were scattered on the grass,
And grape-stalks but half bare, and remnants more,
Sweet-smelling, whose pure kinds I could not know.
Still was more plenty than the fabled horn
Thrice emptied could pour forth, at banqueting
For Proserpine returned to her own fields,
Where the white heifers low. And appetite
More yearning than on Earth I ever felt
Growing within, I ate deliciously;
And, after not long, thirsted, for thereby
Stood a cool vessel of transparent juice
Sipped by the wandered bee, the which I took,

And, pledging all the mortals of the world,
And all the dead whose names are in our lips,
Drank. That full draught is parent of my theme.
No Asian poppy nor elixir fine
Of the soon-fading jealous Caliphat;
No poison gendered in close monkish cell,
To thin the scarlet conclave of old men,
Could so have rapt unwilling life away.
Among the fragrant husks and berries crushed,
Upon the grass I struggled hard against
The domineering potion; but in vain:
The cloudy swoon came on, and down I sank,
Like a Silenus on an antique vase.
How long I slumbered 'tis a chance to guess.
When sense of life returned, I started up
As if with wings; but the fair trees were gone,
The mossy mound and arbour were no more . . .

TIME AND THE GARDEN

The spring has darkened with activity.
The future gathers in vine, bush, and tree:
Persimmon, walnut, loquat, fig, and grape,
Degrees and kinds of color, taste, and shape.
These will advance in their due series, space
The season like a tranquil dwelling-place.
And yet excitement swells me, vein by vein:
I long to crowd the little garden, gain
Its sweetness in my hand and crush it small
And taste it in a moment, time and all!
These trees, whose slow growth measures off my years,
I would expand to greatness. No one hears,
And I am still retarded in duress!
And this is like that other restlessness
To seize the greatness not yet fairly earned,
One which the tougher poets have discerned –
Gascoigne, Ben Jonson, Greville, Raleigh, Donne,
Poets who wrote great poems, one by one,
And spaced by many years, each line an act
Through which few labor, which no men retract.
This passion is the scholar's heritage,
The imposition of a busy age,
The passion to condense from book to book
Unbroken wisdom in a single look,
Though we know well that when this fix the head,
The mind's immortal, but the man is dead.

MYSELF

There is a garden, grey
    With mists of autumntide;
Under the giant boughs,
    Stretched green on every side,

Along the lonely paths,
    A little child like me,
With face, with hands, like mine,
    Plays ever silently;

On, on, quite silently,
    When I am there alone,
Turns not his head; lifts not his eyes;
    Heeds not as he plays on.

After the birds are flown
    From singing in the trees,
When all is grey, all silent,
    Voices, and winds, and bees;

And I am there alone:
    Forlornly, silently,
Plays in the evening garden
    Myself with me.

THE GARDEN OF EPICURUS

That Garden of sedate Philosophy
Once flourished, fenced from passion and mishap,
A shining spot upon a shaggy map;
Where mind and body, in fair junction free,
Luted their joyful concord; like the tree
From root to flowering twigs a flowing sap.
Clear Wisdom found in tended Nature's lap,
Of gentlemen the happy nursery.
That Garden would on light supremest verge,
Were the long drawing of an equal breath
Healthful for Wisdom's head, her heart, her aims.
Our world which for its Babels wants a scourge,
And for its wilds a husbandman, acclaims
The crucifix that came of Nazareth.

THE GARDEN OF WRITING

I think you feel, Antoine, that, of us two
Working here in this garden, it is you
Who's busier – what different songs you'd sing
If, just for two days, freed from gardening,
Suddenly turned a poet and a wit,
You undertook to polish up a bit
Of writing which would deal with matters most
Trivial without stooping (for the cost
Of treating littleness is that one sinks)
Would turn dry thistles into roses and pinks
And confer elegance and dignity
On the discourses of rusticity.

But soon returning from these labors, sore
And dry, the color of your face far more
Tanned than by all the sun and windy air
Of over twenty years, you might declare
As you take up again your rake and shovel
"I'd rather lay a hundred acres level
Than, following mad visions to exhaust
Myself among the clouds, absurdly lost,
And to conjoin words that are out of tune,
Here in this garden, take bites of the moon."

Come, let an idle man, Antoine, explain
What is hard work and what exhaustion's pain.
Man on earth, anxious and beset, at best,
Must always labor, even while at rest;
Fatigue dogs him. It is in vain the nine
Deceitful Muses promise, in their fine
Retreats, repose to poets in the shade:
In these most tranquil woods expressly made
For them, all cadence, rhyme, caesura, stress,
Rhythm well-tuned and full expressiveness –
Witches whose love takes them with charms at first
Eat them up soon with weariness and thirst.
Endlessly following these elusive fays
Each Orpheus gasps for breath beneath his bays.

In torment each one of these poets' minds
Takes pleasure, and some joy in hardship finds
But no fatigue could ever be so tough
As the dumb, tedious leisure of the rough
Man without learning locked yet in the cave
Of his stupidity, the willing slave
Of lazy indolence, must, I should guess,
Bear, in the tedium of his idleness
The heaviest burden one can quite recall
Of having nothing much to do at all.

NICOLAS BOILEAU   91
TRANSLATED BY JOHN HOLLANDER

NO BARREN LEAVES

    Near some fair Town, I'd have a private Seat,
Built Uniform, not Little, nor too Great:
Better, if on a Rising Ground it stood;
Fields on this side, on that a Neighbouring Wood.
It shou'd within no other Things contain,
But what were Useful, Necessary, Plain:
Methinks 'tis Nauseous, and I'd ne'er endure
The needless Pomp of Gaudy Furniture.
A little Garden, Grateful to the Eye,
And a Cool Rivulet run murm'ring by:
On whose delicious Banks a stately Row
Of Shady Limes, or Sycamores, shou'd grow:
At th' End of which a silent Study plac'd,
Shou'd be with all the Noblest Authors Grac'd:
Horace, and *Virgil*, in whose Mighty Lines
Immortal Wit, and Solid Learning shines;
Sharp *Juvenal*, and Am'rous *Ovid* too,
Who all the Turns of Loves soft Passion knew;
He that with Judgment reads his charming Lines,
In which strong Art, with stronger Nature joyns,
Must grant his Fancy does the best Excel,
His Thoughts so tender, and Exprest so well;
With all those Moderns, Men of steady Sense,
Esteem'd for Learning, and for Eloquence.
In some of these, as Fancy shou'd Advise,

I'd always take my Morning Exercise:
For sure no Minutes bring us more Content,
Than those in Pleasing, Useful Studies spent.

GARDENS AND SEASONS

All the seasons run their race
In this quiet resting place ...

AUSTIN DOBSON, "A GARDEN SONG"

SPRING IN THE GARDEN

Ah, cannot the curled shoots of the larkspur that you
    loved so,
Cannot the spiny poppy that no winter kills
Instruct you how to return through the thawing
    ground and the thin snow
Into this April sun that is driving the mist between the
    hills?

A good friend to the monkshood in a time of need
You were, and the lupine's friend as well;
But I see the lupine lift the ground like a tough weed
And the earth over the monkshood swell,

And I fear that not a root in all this heaving sea
Of land, has nudged you where you lie, has found
Patience and time to direct you, numb and stupid as
    you still must be
From your first winter underground.

LATE SPRING

At length the finished garden to the view
Its vistas opens and its alleys green.
Snatched through the verdant maze, the hurried eye
Distracted wanders; now the bowery walk
Of covert close, where scarce a speck of day
Falls on the lengthened gloom, protracted sweeps;
Now meets the bending sky, the river now
Dimpling along, the breezy ruffled lake,
The forest darkening round, the glittering spire,
The ethereal mountain, and the distant main.
But why so far excursive? when at hand,
Along these blushing borders bright with dew,
And in yon mingled wilderness of flowers,
Fair-handed Spring unbosoms every grace –
Throws out the snow-drop and the crocus first,
The daisy, primrose, violet darkly blue,
And polyanthus of unnumbered dyes;
The yellow wall-flower, stained with iron brown,
And lavish stock, that scents the garden round:
From the soft wing of vernal breezes shed,
Anemones; auriculas, enriched
With shining meal o'er all their velvet leaves;
And full ranunculus of glowing red.
Then comes the tulip-race, where beauty plays
Her idle freaks: from family diffused

To family, as flies the father-dust,
The varied colours run; and, while they break
On the charmed eye, the exulting florist marks
With secret pride the wonders of his hand.

❧

THUNDER IN THE GARDEN

When the boughs of the garden hang heavy with rain
And the blackbird reneweth his song,
And the thunder departing yet rolleth again,
I remember the ending of wrong.

When the day that was dusk while his death was aloof
Is ending wide-gleaming and strange
For the clearness of all things beneath the world's roof,
I call back the wild chance and the change.

For once we twain sat through the hot afternoon
While the rain held aloof for a while,
Till she, the soft-clad, for the glory of June
Changed all with the change of her smile.

For her smile was of longing, no longer of glee,
And her fingers, entwined with mine own,
With caresses unquiet sought kindness of me
For the gift that I never had known.

Then down rushed the rain, and the voice of the thunder
Smote dumb all the sound of the street,
And I to myself was grown nought but a wonder,
As she leaned down my kisses to meet.

That she craved for my lips that had craved her so often,
And the hand that had trembled to touch,
That the tears filled her eyes I had hoped not to soften
In this world was a marvel too much.

It was dusk 'mid the thunder, dusk e'en as the night,
When first brake out our love like the storm,
But no night-hour was it, and back came the light
While our hands with each other were warm.

And her smile killed with kisses, came back as at first
As she rose up and led me along,
And out to the garden, where nought was athirst,
And the blackbird renewing his song.

Earth's fragrance went with her, as in the wet grass
Her feet little hidden were set;
She bent down her head, 'neath the roses to pass,
And her arm with the lily was wet.

In the garden we wandered while day waned apace
And the thunder was dying aloof;
Till the moon o'er the minster-wall lifted his face,
And grey gleamed out the lead of the roof.

Then we turned from the blossoms, and cold were they
     grown
In the trees the wind westering moved;
Till over the threshold back fluttered her gown,
And in the dark house was I loved.

BANAL SOJOURN

Two wooden tubs of blue hydrangeas stand at the foot
    of the stone steps.
The sky is a blue gum streaked with rose. The trees are
    black.
The grackles crack their throats of bone in the smooth
    air.
Moisture and heat have swollen the garden into a slum
    of bloom.
Pardie! Summer is like a fat beast, sleepy in mildew,
Our old bane, green and bloated, serene, who cries,
"That bliss of stars, that princox of evening heaven!"
    reminding of seasons,
When radiance came running down, slim through the
    bareness.
And so it is one damns that green shade at the bottom
    of the land.
For who can care at the wigs despoiling the Satan ear?
And who does not seek the sky unfuzzed, soaring to
    the princox?
One has a malady, here, a malady. One feels a malady.

THE GARDEN
On prospect of a fine day in early autumn

How kind, how secret, now the sun
Will bless this garden frost has won,
And touch once more, as once it used,
The furled boughs by cold bemused.
Though summered brilliance had but room
In blossom, now the leaves will bloom
Their time, and take from milder sun
An unreviving benison.

No marbles whitely gaze among
These paths where gilt the late pear hung:
But branches interlace to frame
The avenue of stately flame
Where yonder, far more bold and pure
Than marble, gleams the sycamore,
Of argent torse and cunning shaft
Propped nobler than the sculptor's craft.

The hand that crooked upon the spade
Here plucked the peach, and thirst allayed;
Here lovers paused before the kiss,
Instructed of what ripeness is:
Where all who came might stand to prove
The grace of this imperial grove,
Now jay and cardinal debate,
Like twin usurpers, the ruined state.

But he who sought, not love, but peace
In such rank plot could take no ease:
Now poised between the two alarms
Of summer's lusts and winter's harms,
Only for him these precincts wait
In sacrament that can translate
All things that fed luxurious sense
From appetite to innocence.

THE GARDEN IN SEPTEMBER

   Now thin mists temper the slow-ripening beams
Of the September sun: his golden gleams
On gaudy flowers shine, that prank the rows
Of high-grown hollyhocks, and all tall shows
That Autumn flaunteth in his bushy bowers;
Where tomtits, hanging from the drooping heads
Of giant sunflowers, peck the nutty seeds;
And in the feathery aster bees on wing
Seize and set free the honied flowers,
Till thousand stars leap with their visiting:
While ever across the path mazily flit,
Unpiloted in the sun,
The dreamy butterflies
With dazzling colours powdered and soft glooms,
White, black and crimson stripes, and peacock eyes,
Or on chance flowers sit,
With idle effort plundering one by one
The nectaries of deepest-throated blooms.

   With gentle flaws the western breeze
Into the garden saileth,
Scarce here and there stirring the single trees,
For his sharpness he vaileth:
So long a comrade of the bearded corn,
Now from the stubbles whence the shocks are borne,

O'er dewy lawns he turns to stray,
As mindful of the kisses and soft play
Wherewith he enamoured the light-hearted May,
Ere he deserted her;
Lover of fragrance, and too late repents;
Nor more of heavy hyacinth now may drink,
Nor spicy pink,
Nor summer's rose, nor garnered lavender,
But the few lingering scents
Of streakèd pea, and gillyflower, and stocks
Of courtly purple, and aromatic phlox.

And at all times to hear are drowsy tones
Of dizzy flies, and humming drones,
With sudden flap of pigeon wings in the sky,
Or the wild cry
Of thirsty rooks, that scour ascare
The distant blue, to watering as they fare
With creaking pinions, or – on business bent,
If aught their ancient polity displease, –
Come gathering to their colony, and there
Settling in ragged parliament,
Some stormy council hold in the high trees.

AN OCTOBER GARDEN

In my Autumn garden I was fain
    To mourn among my scattered roses;
    Alas for that last rosebud that uncloses
To Autumn's languid sun and rain
When all the world is on the wane!
    Which has not felt the sweet constraint of June,
    Nor heard the nightingale in tune.

Broad-faced asters by my garden walk,
    You are but coarse compared with roses:
    More choice, more dear that rosebud which
        uncloses,
Faint-scented, pinched, upon its stalk,
That least and last which cold winds balk;
    A rose it is though least and last of all,
    A rose to me though at the fall.

AUTUMN GARDEN
(*Florence*)

To the ghostly garden to the laurel mute
Green garlands shorn
To the autumnal country
Now a last salute!
Up the parched falling lawns
Harsh scarlet in the sun's last rays
Struggles a torn
Deep-throated roar – life crying far away:
It cries to the dying sun that sheds
Dark blood on the flower-beds.
A brass band saws
The air: the river's gone
Between its golden sands: in a great calm
The dazzling statues that the bridgehead bore
Are turned away: there's nothing any more.
Out of profound silence, something like
A chorus soft and grand,
Longing, soars to the terrace where I stand:
And in redolence of laurel,
Of laurel languorous, laurel piercing, where
Those statues in the sunset loom immortal,
She appears, present there.

DINO CAMPANA   109
TRANSLATED BY JOHN FREDERICK NIMS

NOVEMBER
Impression

A weft of leafless spray
Woven fine against the gray
Of the autumnal day,
And blurred along those ghostly garden tops
Clusters of berries crimson as the drops
That my heart bleeds when I remember
How often, in how many a far November,
Of childhood and my children's childhood I was glad,
With the wild rapture of the Fall,
Of all the beauty, and of all
The ruin, now so intolerably sad.

FROST

Therefore, lest this inclement friend should maim
Your valued plants, plunge pots within a frame
Sunk deep in sand or ashes to the rim,
Warm nursery when nights and days are grim;
But in the long brown borders where the frost
May hold its mischievous and midnight play
And all your winnings of the months be lost
In one short gamble when the dice are tossed
Finally and forever in few hours,
– The chance your skill, the stake your flowers, –
Throw bracken, never sodden, light and tough
In almost weightless armfuls down, to rest
Buoyant on tender and frost-fearing plants;
Or set the wattled hurdle in a square
Protective, where the north-east wind is gruff,
As sensitive natures seek for comfort lest
Th'assault of life be more than they can bear,
And find an end, not in timidity
But death's decisive certainty.

V. SACKVILLE-WEST

A WINTER EDEN

A winter garden in an alder swamp,
Where conies now come out to sun and romp,
As near a paradise as it can be
And not melt snow or start a dormant tree.

It lifts existence on a plane of snow
One level higher than the earth below,
One level nearer heaven overhead,
And last year's berries shining scarlet red.

It lifts a gaunt luxuriating beast
Where he can stretch and hold his highest feast
On some wild apple tree's young tender bark,
What well may prove the year's high girdle mark.

So near to paradise all pairing ends:
Here loveless birds now flock as winter friends,
Content with bud-inspecting. They presume
To say which buds are leaf and which are bloom.

A feather-hammer gives a double knock.
This Eden day is done at two o'clock.
An hour of winter day might seem too short
To make it worth life's while to wake and sport.

SONG

A spirit haunts the year's last hours
Dwelling amid these yellowing bowers:
    To himself he talks;
For at eventide, listening earnestly,
At his work you may hear him sob and sigh
    In the walks;
    Earthward he boweth the heavy stalks
Of the mouldering flowers:
  Heavily hangs the broad sunflower
    Over its grave i' the earth so chilly;
  Heavily hangs the hollyhock,
    Heavily hangs the tiger-lily.

The air is damp, and hushed, and close,
As a sick man's room when he taketh repose
    An hour before death;
My very heart faints and my whole soul grieves
At the moist rich smell of the rotting leaves,
    And the breath
    Of the fading edges of box beneath,
And the year's last rose.
  Heavily hangs the broad sunflower
    Over its grave i' the earth so chilly;
  Heavily hangs the hollyhock,
    Heavily hangs the tiger-lily.

IN WINTER

A garden that recalls the past,
but in it I stack
driftwood for fuel –
hardly the kind of year-end
I used to know.

TRANSLATED BY BURTON WATSON

FLOWERS

On a radiant summer morning
The garden paths I sought:
The flowers whisper and murmur —
I walk in silent thought.

The flowers whisper and murmur
With pity, as soft as they can:
"Don't be angry with our sister,
You pale and sorrowful man!"

HEINRICH HEINE
TRANSLATED BY HAL DRAPER

FLOWERING PLUMS

All dressed alike in white silk skirts and kerchiefs.
Quiet purity and bright adornment were their offerings.
They saw I paid them no attention.
Their cold chastity cleaned my bones, sobered my heart.
From now on, all my life I'll think no evil thoughts.
Some flowering pear trees look as if they were boasting.
Next to them is a single plum,
Her appearance sad as though stifling a sigh.
I ask, but she won't tell the reason.
Alone I walk around her a hundred times, till dusk.
Suddenly I recall having passed this tree before,
Just when the fragrance was first budding.
I was too drunk to notice,
Failed to see the jade branches holding frosty blossoms!
For your sake I shed a rain of tears,
Unable to turn back the sun's chariot.
When the east wind blows, she still looks unhappy;
Spreading far, the night air wraps her.

On an icy platter in summer they serve the purple fruit,
    full ripe.
Out of shame I send it back without eating, thinking of
    the blossoms.

HAN YÜ   117
TRANSLATED BY HANS H. FRANKEL

THE LESSON OF THE FLOWERS

'Twas morning, and the Lord of day
   Had shed his light o'er Shiraz' towers,
Where bulbuls trill their love-lorn lay
   To serenade the maiden flowers.

Like them, oppressed by love's sweet pain
   I wander in a garden fair;
And there, to cool my throbbing brain,
   I woo the perfumed morning air.

The damask rose with beauty gleams,
   Its face all bathed in ruddy light,
And shines like some bright star that beams
   From out the sombre veil of night.

The very bulbul, as the glow
   Of pride and passion warms its breast,
Forgets awhile its former woe
   In pride that conquers love's unrest.

The sweet narcissus opes its eye,
   A tear-drop glistening on the lash,
As though 'twere gazing piteously
   Upon the tulip's bleeding gash.

118

The lily seemed to menace me,
    And showed its curved and quivering blade,
While every frail anemone
    A gossip's open mouth displayed.

And here and there a graceful group
    Of flowers, like men who worship wine,
Each raising up his little stoup
    To catch the dew-drop's draught divine.

And others yet like Hebes stand,
    Their dripping vases downward turned,
As if dispensing to the band
    The wine for which their hearts had burned.

This moral it is mine to sing:
    Go learn a lesson of the flowers;
Joy's season is in life's young spring,
    Then seize, like them, the fleeting hours.

OF ROSES AND HYACINTHS

    I cannot all the *Species* rehearse
Of Roses, in the narrow bounds of Verse.
Some curl'd, some wav'd about the top are found,
And others with a thousand leaves are crown'd
Through which the flaming colours do appear.
Others are single – not t'insist on here
Either the Damask or *Numidian* Rose,
Or *Citrus*, which in *Lusitania* grows.
Roses unarm'd, if you the earth prepare,
May be produc'd, but that in danger are,
Because unguarded, for what excellence
Can be secure on earth without defence? ...
    These flow'rs are quickly subject to decay,
And when *Orion* shines, they fade away.
In Pots the candid *Hyacinths* remain
Entire, which from their tub'rous roots obtain
Another home; our Merchants those of late
From the far distant Indies did translate.
Their station first in *Italy* they had;
And then to *Rome*, and *Latium* were convey'd,
From whence all *Europe* has been furnish'd where
In every *Garden* they now domineer,
Not only boasting of the native Snow.
Which decks their front, but of their Odours too.

TRANSLATED BY JOHN EVELYN

THE POPPY

Sopha'd on silk, amid her charm-built towers,
Her meads of asphodel, and amaranth bowers,
Where Sleep and Silence guard the soft abodes,
In sullen apathy PAPAVER nods.
Faint o'er her couch in scintillating streams
Pass the thin forms of Fancy and of Dreams;
Froze by inchantment on the velvet ground
Fair youths and beauteous ladies glitter round;
On crystal pedestals they seem to sigh,
Bend the meek knee, and lift the imploring eye.
– And now the Sorceress bares her shrivel'd hand,
And circles thrice in air her ebon wand;
Flush'd with new life descending statues talk,
The pliant marble softening as they walk;
With deeper sobs reviving lovers breathe,
Fair bosoms rise, and soft hearts pant beneath;
With warmer lips relentless damsels speak,
And kindling blushes tinge the Parian cheek;
To viewless lutes aërial voices sing,
And hovering Loves are heard on rustling wing.
– She waves her wand again! – fresh horrors seize
Their stiffening limbs, their vital currents freeze;
By each cold nymph her marble lover lies,
And iron slumbers seal their glassy eyes.

ERASMUS DARWIN   121

TO A BED OF TULIPS

Bright Tulips, we do know,
You had your comming hither;
And Fading-time do's show,
That Ye must quickly wither.

Your *Sister-hoods* may stay,
And smile here for your houre;
But dye ye must away:
Even as the meanest Flower.

Come Virgins then, and see
Your frailties; and bemone ye;
For lost like these, 'twill be,
As Time had never known ye.

THE TULIP BED

The May sun – whom
all things imitate –
that glues small leaves to
the wooden trees
shone from the sky
through bluegauze clouds
upon the ground.
Under the leafy trees
where the suburban streets
lay crossed,
with houses on each corner,
tangled shadows had begun
to join
the roadway and the lawns.
With excellent precision
the tulip bed
inside the iron fence
upreared its gaudy
yellow, white and red,
rimmed round with grass,
reposedly.

THE ROSE

June of the iris and the rose.
The rose not English as we fondly think.
Anacreon and Bion sang the rose;
And Rhodes the isle whose very name means rose
Struck roses on her coins;
Pliny made lists and Roman libertines
Made wreaths to wear among the flutes and wines;
The young Crusaders found the Syrian rose
Springing from Saracenic quoins,
And China opened her shut gate
To let her roses through, and Persian shrines
Of poetry and painting gave the rose.

The air of June is velvet with her scent,
The realm of June is splendid with her state.
Asia and Europe to our island lent
These parents of our rose,
Yet Albion took her name from her white rose
Not from her cliffs, some say. So let it be.
We know the dog-rose, flinging free
Whip-lashes in the hedgerow, starred with pale
Shell blossom as a Canterbury Tale,
The candid English genius, fresh and pink
As Chaucer made us think,
Singing of adolescent meads in May.

That's not the rose in her true character;
She's a voluptuary; think of her
Wine-dark and heavy-scented of the South,
Stuck in a cap or dangled from a mouth
As soft as her own petals. That's the rose!
No sentimentalist, no maiden sweet,
Appealing, half-forlorn,
But deep and old and cunning in deceit,
Offering promises too near the thorn.
She is an expert and experienced woman
Wearing her many faces
Pleasing to different men in different places;
She plays the madrigal when moist with dew
To charm the English in their artless few,
But at her wiser older broad remove
Remains an Asiatic and a Roman,
Accomplice of the centuries and love.

Dangerous beauty we have sometimes seen,
Dangerous moments we have sometimes had.
Thus I saw floating in a sunken pool
A pavement of red roses in Baghdad.

A floating floor of dark beheaded blood
Between blue tiles that feigned to look so cool,
And that was beauty, sunk in liquid floor
Of roses and of water red as war,

125

But other visions took me on their flood
To other blood-red points where I had been:

St. Mark's in Venice on an Easter-day
Deep as the petals of Arabian rose,
When a great Cardinal in robes arose
Tremendous in the pulpit, and began
"Così diceva lo scrittor pagan" . . .
Virgil a living presence in the church;
Lambent mosaics, tarnished in their gold,
And all things heavy with their age, so old
They seemed as distant as my own lost search.

Those blood-red roses floating in the pool,
That blood-red lamp above the altar slung,
Were they identical, or I a fool?
God's lamp His own red rose, where censers swung?

THE FLOWER'S NAME

I

Here's the garden she walked across,
   Arm in my arm, such a short while since:
Hark, now I push its wicket, the moss
   Hinders the hinges and makes them wince!
She must have reached this shrub ere she turned,
   As back with that murmur the wicket swung;
For she laid the poor snail, my chance foot spurned,
   To feed and forget it the leaves among.

II

Down this side of the gravel-walk
   She went while her robe's edge brushed the box:
And here she paused in her gracious talk
   To point me a moth on the milk-white phlox.
Roses, ranged in valiant row,
   I will never think that she passed you by!
She loves you noble roses, I know;
   But yonder, see, where the rock-plants lie!

III

This flower she stopped at, finger on lip,
    Stooped over, in doubt, as settling its claim;
Till she gave me, with pride to make no slip,
    Its soft meandering Spanish name:
What a name! Was it love or praise?
    Speech half-asleep or song half-awake?
I must learn Spanish, one of these days,
    Only for that slow sweet name's sake.

IV

Roses, if I live and do well,
    I may bring her, one of these days,
To fix you fast with as fine a spell,
    Fit you each with his Spanish phrase;
But do not detain me now; for she lingers
    There, like sunshine over the ground,
And ever I see her soft white fingers
    Searching after the bud she found.

Flower, you Spaniard, look that you grow not,
  Stay as you are and be loved for ever!
Bud, if I kiss you 'tis that you blow not:
  Mind, the shut pink mouth opens never!
For while it pouts, her fingers wrestle,
  Twinkling the audacious leaves between
Till round they turn and down they nestle –
  Is not the dear mark still to be seen?

VI

Where I find her not, beauties vanish;
  Whither I follow her, beauties flee;
Is there no method to tell her in Spanish
  June's twice June since she breathed it with me?
Come, bud, show me the least of her traces,
  Treasure my lady's lightest footfall!
– Ah, you may flout and turn up your faces –
  Roses, you are not so fair after all!

WEEDS

   The pigrush, the poverty grass,
The bindweed's stranglehold morning glories,
   The dog blow and ninety-joints –
They ask so little of us to start with,
   Just a crack in the asphalt,
Or a subway grate with an hour of weak light.
   One I know has put down roots
As far as a corpse is buried, its storage stem
   As big as my leg. That one's called
Man-under-ground. That one was my grudge.

   And suddenly now this small
Unlooked for joy. Where did *it* come from,
   With these pale shoots
And drooping lavender bell? Persistent
   Intruder, whether or not
I want you, you've hidden in the heart's
   Overworked subsoil. Hacked at
Or trampled on, may you divide and spread,
   Just as, all last night,
The wind scattered a milkweed across the sky.

WHAT THE FLOWERS SAID

Again the violet bent double has arrived beside the lily, again the ruby-clad rose is tearing her gown to shreds;

Again our green-gowned ones have gaily arrived from beyond the world swift as the wind, drunken and stalking and joyous.

The standard-bearing cypress went off and consumed autumn with rage, and from the mountain-top the sweet-featured anemone showed its face.

The hyacinth said to the jasmine, "Peace be upon you"; the latter replied, "Upon you be peace; come, lad, into the meadow!"

A Sufi on every side, having attained some favour, clapping hands like the plane-tree, dancing like the zephyr;

The bud, concealing its face like veiled ladies – the breeze draws aside its chaddur saying, "Unveil your face, good friend!"

The friend is in this quarter of ours, water in this our stream; lotus in your finery, why are you athirst and pale?

Sour-faced winter has departed, that joy-slayer has been slain; swift-footed jasmine, long may you live!

The busy narcissus winked at the verdure; the verdure understood its words and said, "Yours is the command."

The clove said to the willow, "I am in hope of you"; the willow answered, "My bachelor apartment is your private chamber – welcome!"

The apple said, "Orange, why are you puckered?" The orange replied, "I do not show myself off for fear of the evil eye."

The ringdove came cooing, "Where is that friend?" The sweet-noted nightingale pointed him to the rose.

Beside the world's springtide there is a secret spring; moon-cheeked and sweet of mouth, give wine, O saki!

Moon rising in the shadows of darkness, the light of whose lamp vanquishes the sun at noon!

Several words yet remain unsaid, but it is unseasonably late; whatever was omitted in the night I will complete tomorrow.

❧

COME INTO THE GARDEN, MAUD

I

Come into the garden, Maud,
   For the black bat, night, has flown,
Come into the garden, Maud,
   I am here at the gate alone;
And the woodbine spices are wafted abroad,
   And the musk of the rose is blown.

II

For a breeze of morning moves,
   And the planet of Love is on high,
Beginning to faint in the light that she loves
   On a bed of daffodil sky,
To faint in the light of the sun she loves,
   To faint in his light, and to die.

III

All night have the roses heard
   The flute, violin, bassoon;
All night has the casement jessamine stirred
   To the dancers dancing in tune;
Till a silence fell with the waking bird,
   And a hush with the setting moon.

IV

I said to the lily, "There is but one
    With whom she has heart to be gay.
When will the dancers leave her alone?
    She is weary of dance and play."
Now half to the setting moon are gone,
    And half to the rising day;
Low on the sand and loud on the stone
    The last wheel echoes away.

V

I said to the rose, "The brief night goes
    In babble and revel and wine.
O young lord-lover, what sighs are those,
    For one that will never be thine?
But mine, but mine," so I swore to the rose,
    "For ever and ever, mine."

VI

And the soul of the rose went into my blood,
    As the music clashed in the hall;
And long by the garden lake I stood,
    For I heard your rivulet fall
From the lake to the meadow and on to the wood,
    Our wood, that is dearer than all;

VII

From the meadow your walks have left so sweet
    That whenever a March-wind sighs
He sets the jewel-print of your feet
    In violets blue as your eyes,
To the woody hollows in which we meet
    And the valleys of Paradise.

VIII

The slender acacia would not shake
    One long milk-bloom on the tree;
The white lake-blossom fell into the lake
    As the pimpernel dozed on the lea;
But the rose was awake all night for your sake,
    Knowing your promise to me;
The lilies and roses were all awake,
    They sighed for the dawn and thee.

IX

Queen rose of the rosebud garden of girls,
    Come hither, the dances are done,
In gloss of satin and glimmer of pearls,
    Queen lily and rose in one;
Shine out, little head, sunning over with curls,
    To the flowers, and be their sun.

There has fallen a splendid tear
    From the passion-flower at the gate.
She is coming, my dove, my dear;
    She is coming, my life, my fate;
The red rose cries, "She is near, she is near;"
    And the white rose weeps, "She is late;"
The larkspur listens, "I hear, I hear;"
    And the lily whispers, "I wait."

GARDENERS

Out in the garden,
Out in the windy, swinging dark,
Under the trees and over the flower-beds,
Over the grass and under the hedge border,
Someone is sweeping, sweeping,
Some old gardener.
Out in the windy, swinging dark,
Someone is secretly putting in order,
Someone is creeping, creeping.

KATHERINE MANSFIELD
"OUT IN THE GARDEN"

GARDENER

Loveliest flowers, though crooked in their border,
And glorious fruit, dangling from ill-pruned boughs –
Be sure the gardener had not eye enough
To wheel a barrow between the broadest gates
Without a clumsy scraping.

Yet none could think it simple awkwardness;
And when he stammered of a garden-guardian,
That the smooth lawns came by angelic favour,
The pinks and pears in spite of his own blunders,
They nudged at this conceit.

Well, he had something, though he called it nothing –
As ass's wit, a hairy-belly shrewdness
That would appraise the intentions of the angel
By the very difference of his own confusion,
And bring the most to pass.

GARDENER

Under the window, on a dusty ledge,
He peers among the spider webs for seed.
He wonders, groping, if the spiders spun
Beneath that window after all. Perhaps
His eyes are spiders, and new veils are dropped
Each winter and summer morning in the brain.
He sees but silken-dimly, though the ends
Of his white fingers feel more things than are:
More delicate webs, and sundry bags of seed.
That flicker at the window is a wren.
She taps the pane with a neat tail, and scolds.
He knows her there, and hears her – far away,
As if an insect sang in a tree. Whereat
The shelf he fumbles on is distant, too,
And his bent arm is longer than an arm.
Something between his fingers brings him back:
An envelope that rustles, and he reads:
"The coreopsis." He does not delay.
Down from the rafter where they always hang
He shoulders rake and hoe, and shuffles out.

The sun is warm and thick upon the path,
But he goes lightly, under a broad straw
None knows the age of. They are watching him
From upper windows as his slippered feet
Avoid the aster and nasturtium beds
Where he is not to meddle. His preserve
Is further, and no stranger touches it.
Yesterday he was planting larkspur there.
He works the ground the hoes the larkspur out,
Pressing the coreopsis gently in.
With an old hose he plays a quavering stream,
Then shuffles back with the tools and goes to supper.

Over his bowl of milk, wherein he breaks
Five brittle crackers, drifts the question: "Uncle,
What have you planted for the summer coming?"

"Why – hollyhocks," he murmurs; and they smile.

THE GARDENER

The gardener does not love to talk,
He makes me keep the gravel walk;
And when he puts his tools away,
He locks the door and takes the key.

Away behind the currant row
Where no one else but cook may go,
Far in the plots, I see him dig,
Old and serious, brown and big.

He digs the flowers, green, red, and blue,
Nor wishes to be spoken to.
He digs the flowers and cuts the hay,
And never seems to want to play.

Silly gardener! summer goes,
And winter comes with pinching toes,
When in the garden bare and brown
You must lay your barrow down.

Well now, and while the summer stays,
To profit by these garden days,
O how much wiser you would be
To play at Indian wars with me!

GARDENS NO EMBLEMS

Man with a scythe: the torrent of his swing
Finds its own level; and is not hauled back
But gathers fluently, like water rising
Behind the watergates that close a lock.

The gardener eased his foot into a boot;
Which action like the mower's had its mould,
Being itself a sort of taking root,
Feeling for lodgment in the leather's fold.

But forms of thought move in another plane
Whose matrices no natural forms afford
Unless subjected to prodigious strain:
Say, light proceeding edgewise, like a sword.

THE GARDENER'S LESSON

Gard.　Go bind thou up young dangling apricocks,
Which like unruly children make their sire
Stoop with oppression of their prodigal weight;
Give some supportance to the bending twigs.
Go thou, and like an executioner
Cut off the heads of [too] fast growing sprays,
That look too lofty in our commonwealth:
All must be even in our government.
You thus employed, I will go root away
The noisome weeds which without profit suck
The soil's fertility from wholesome flowers.
　Man.　Why should we in the compass of a pale
Keep law and form and due proportion,
Showing as in a model our firm estate,
When our sea-walled garden, the whole land,
Is full of weeds, her fairest flowers chok'd up,
Her fruit-trees all unprun'd, her hedges ruin'd,
Her knots disordered, and her wholesome herbs
Swarming with caterpillars?
　Gard.　　　　　　　　　Hold thy peace.
He that hath suffered this disordered spring
Hath now himself met with the fall of leaf.
The weeds which his broad-spreading leaves did
　　shelter,
That seem'd in eating him to hold him up,

Are pluck'd up root and all by Bullingbrook,
I mean the Earl of Wiltshire, Bushy, Green.
   Man.   What, are they dead?
   Gard.   They are; and Bullingbrook
Hath seiz'd the wasteful King. O, what pity is it
That he had not so trimm'd and dress'd his land
As we this garden! [We] at time of year
Do wound the bark, the skin of our fruit-trees,
Lest being over-proud in sap and blood,
With too much riches it confound itself;
Had he done so to great and growing men,
They might have liv'd to bear and he to taste
Their fruits of duty. Superfluous branches
We lop away, that bearing boughs may live;
Had he done so, himself had borne the crown,
Which waste of idle hours hath quite thrown down.

A GIRL'S GARDEN

A neighbor of mine in the village
  Likes to tell how one spring
When she was a girl on the farm, she did
  A childlike thing.

One day she asked her father
  To give her a garden plot
To plant and tend and reap herself,
  And he said, "Why not?"

In casting about for a corner
  He thought of an idle bit
Of walled-off ground where a shop had stood,
  And he said, "Just it."

And he said, "That ought to make you
  An *i*deal one-girl farm,
And give you a chance to put some strength
  On your slim-jim arm."

It was not enough of a garden,
  Her father said, to plough;
So she had to work it all by hand,
  But she don't mind now.

She wheeled the dung in the wheelbarrow
    Along a stretch of road;
But she always ran away and left
    Her not-nice load,

And hid from anyone passing.
    And then she begged the seed.
She says she thinks she planted one
    Of all things but weed.

A hill each of potatoes,
    Radishes, lettuce, peas,
Tomatoes, beets, beans, pumpkins, corn,
    And even fruit trees.

And yes, she has long mistrusted
    That a cider apple tree
In bearing there to-day is hers,
    Or at least may be.

Her crop was a miscellany
    When all was said and done,
A little bit of everything,
    A great deal of none.

Now when she sees in the village
    How village things go,
Just when it seems to come in right,
    She says, "*I* know!

It's as when I was a farmer —"
    Oh, never by way of advice!
And she never sins by telling the tale
    To the same person twice.

THE EMPEROR OF
CHINA SPEAKS

At the heart of all creation
I, the Son of Heaven, dwell;
With my wives and with my trees,
With my animals and ponds,
Which the inmost wall encloses:
Down below my ancestors
Lie in state with all their weapons,
And their crowns upon their heads;
Every one as it is fitting
Dwells in his allotted vault.
Far into the world's deep centre
My majestic tread resounds.
From these green and grassy banks,
Footstools rounded for my comfort,
Silently four equal rivers
East and west and north and south
Flow to irrigate my garden,
Every corner of the world.
Here they mirror the dark eyes,
Gaudy wings of my tame creatures,
Further out, the mottled cities,
Forests wide and dense, dark walls,
Faces of my various peoples.
But my nobles, like the stars,

Dwell around me bearing names
Which I gave to each in token
Of the one and solemn hour
When he rose into my presence,
Wives who were my gifts to them
And their multitude of children;
All the nobles of this earth
Owe their eyes and lips and stature
To my care, a gardener's care.
But between the outer walls
Dwell my peoples, warrior peoples,
Others too that till the fields.
New walls follow and within them
Subjects lately quelled, of ever
Dimmer and more torrid blood,
To the sea, the ultimate wall
That surrounds my realm and me.

TRANSLATED BY MICHAEL HAMBURGER

DIGGING

To-day I think
Only with scents, – scents dead leaves yield,
And bracken, and wild carrot's seed,
And the square mustard field;

Odours that rise
When the spade wounds the root of tree,
Rose, currant, raspberry, or goutweed,
Rhubarb or celery;

The smoke's smell, too,
Flowing from where a bonfire burns
The dead, the waste, the dangerous,
And all to sweetness turns.

It is enough
To smell, to crumble the dark earth,
While the robin sings over again
Sad songs of Autumn mirth.

THE GARDENER TO HIS GOD

"Amazing research proves simple prayer makes
flowers grow many times faster, stronger, larger."
                              Advertisement in The Flower Grower

I pray that the great world's flowering stay as it is,
that larkspur and snapdragon keep to their ordinary size,
and bleedingheart hang in its old way, and Judas tree
stand well below oak, and old oaks color the fall sky.
For the myrtle to keep underfoot, and no rose
to send up a swollen face, I pray simply.

There is no disorder but the heart's. But if love goes
      leaking
outward, if shrubs take up its monstrous stalking,
all greenery is spurred, the snapping lips are
      overgrown,
and over oaks red hearts hang like the sun.
Deliver us from its giant gardening, from walking
all over the earth with no rest from its disproportion.

Let all flowers turn to stone before ever they
        begin to share
love's spaciousness, and faster, stronger, larger
grow from a sweet thought, before any daisy
turns, under love's gibberellic wish, to the day's eye.
Let all blooms take shape from cold laws,
        down from a cold air
let come their small grace or measurable majesty.

For in every place but love the imagination lies
in its limits. Even poems draw back from images
of that one country, on top of whose lunatic stemming
whoever finds himself there must sway and cling
until the high cold God takes pity, and it all dies
down, down into the great world's flowering.

THE GARDENER

Bloom, O my rose!
Bloom there where blows
The vernal, not autumnal, air.
Enough for me
At times to see
A flower an angel ought to wear.

Thy graceful jar
Was rais'd afar
From that which holds my coarser clay,
Yet could thy smile
Warm it awhile
And keep the distance half away.

THE WORK OF
THE GARDEN

Let us divide our labours, thou where choice
Leads thee, or where most needs, whether to wind
The Woodbine round this Arbor, or direct
The clasping ivy where it climb, while I
In yonder Spring of Roses intermixt
With Myrtle, find what to redress till Noon...

JOHN MILTON
FROM *PARADISE LOST*, IX

To build, to plant, whatever you intend,
To rear the Column, or the Arch to bend,
To swell the Terras, or to sink the Grot;
In all, let Nature never be forgot.
But treat the Goddess like a modest fair,
Nor over-dress, nor leave her wholly bare;
Let not each beauty ev'ry where be spy'd,
Where half the skill is decently to hide.
He gains all points, who pleasingly confounds,
Surprizes, varies, and conceals the Bounds.
Consult the Genius of the Place in all;
That tells the Waters or to rise, or fall,
Or helps th' ambitious Hill the heav'n to scale,
Or scoops in circling theatres the Vale,
Calls in the Country, catches opening glades,
Joins willing woods, and varies shades from shades,
Now breaks or now directs, th' intending Lines;
Paints as you plant, and, as you work, designs.

ALEXANDER POPE

TRANSPLANTING

Watching hands transplanting,
Turning and tamping,
Lifting the young plants with two fingers,
Sifting in a palm-full of fresh loam, –
One swift movement, –
Then plumping in the bunched roots,
A single twist of the thumbs, a tamping and turning,
All in one,
Quick on the wooden bench,
A shaking down, while the stem stays straight,
Once, twice, and a faint third thump, –
Into the flat-box it goes,
Ready for the long days under the sloped glass:

The sun warming the fine loam,
The young horns winding and unwinding,
Creaking their thin spines,
The underleaves, the smallest buds
Breaking into nakedness,
The blossoms extending
Out into the sweet air,
The whole flower extending outward,
Stretching and reaching.

ON GRAFTING

If the fresh trunk have sap enough to give
    That each insertive branch may live;
The gardener grafts not only apples there,
    But adds the warden and the pear.
The peach and apricot together grow,
    The cherry and the damson too,
Till he hath made by skilful husbandry
    An entire orchard of one tree.
So lest our paradise perfection want,
    We may as well inoculate as plant.

THE MOWER AGAINST GARDENS

Luxurious man, to bring his vice in use,
    Did after him the world seduce,
And from the fields the flowers and plants allure,
    Where Nature was most plain and pure.
He first enclosed within the gardens square
    A dead and standing pool of air,
And a more luscious earth for them did knead,
    Which stupefied them while it fed.
The pink grew then as double as his mind;
    The nutriment did change the kind.
With strange perfumes he did the roses taint;
    And flowers themselves were taught to paint.
The tulip white did for complexion seek,
    And learned to interline its cheek;
Its onion root they then so high did hold,
    That one was for a meadow sold:
Another world was searched through oceans new,
    To find the marvel of Peru;
And yet these rarities might be allowed
    To man, that sovereign thing and proud,
Had he not dealt between the bark and tree,
    Forbidden mixtures there to see.
No plant now knew the stock from which it came;
    He grafts upon the wild the tame,
That the uncertain and adulterate fruit

Might put the palate in dispute.
His green seraglio has its eunuchs too,
    Lest any tyrant him outdo;
And in the cherry he does Nature vex,
    To procreate without a sex.
'Tis all enforced, the fountain and the grot,
    While the sweet fields do lie forgot,
Where willing Nature does to all dispense
    A wild and fragrant innocence;
And fauns and fairies do the meadows till
    More by their presence than their skill.
Their statues polished by some ancient hand,
    May to adorn the gardens stand;
But, howsoe'er the figures do excel,
    The Gods themselves with us do dwell.

AUTUMNAL WORK

But when the harvest with ripe ears of corn
Grows yellow, and bright *Titan* with his *Twins*
Extends the day, and with his burning heat
Shall scorch the claws of the *Lernæan Crab*,
Then *garlick* join with *onions*, and with *dill*
The *Cerealian poppies*; and, when bound
In bundles, while they're green, to market bring;
And, when your wares are sold, with chearful voice
The praises of propitious *Fortune* found,
And to your gardens hasten back with joy:
And, in new-broken and well-wat'red ground
Sow *basil*, and with weighty cylinders
Compress it, lest the scorching heats pervade
The loose and open dust, and parch the seeds;
Or the small garden-insect, creeping in
By stealth, infest and vex them with its teeth;
Or the rapacious plund'ring ant destroy.
Not only dares the *snail*, wrapt in its shell,
And hairy *palmer-worm*, presume to gnaw
The tender buds and leaves; but, as soon as
The lurid *cabbage*, on its thriving stalk,
Begins to swell, and pale *beet* bulky grows;
And Gard'ner, free from fear, rejoices in
His adult wares, and, now they're ripe, prepares
The sickle to put in; oft-times fierce *Jove*

Does dart his grievous show'rs, and with hail-stones
The labours both of men and beasts destroys:
He, likewise, oft with rains, pregnant with seeds
Pestiferous, bedews them, which produce
Those worms, which to grey *willow-groves*, and *vines*,
Are hurtful; and o'er all the gardens creeps
The caterpiller, which, with pois'nous bite,
Dries up the plants, which, of their comely hair
Bereft, lie mangled with their naked tops,
And with the baneful poison pine and die.

ON PRUNING

Proud of his well-spread walls, he views his trees
That meet (no barren interval between)
With pleasure more than ev'n their fruits afford,
Which, save himself who trains them, none can feel:
These, therefore, are his own peculiar charge;
No meaner hand may discipline the shoots,
None but his steel approach them. What is weak,
Distemper'd, or has lost prolific pow'rs,
Impair'd by age, his unrelenting hand
Dooms to the knife: nor does he spare the soft
And succulent, that feeds its giant growth,
But barren, at th' expence of neighb'ring twigs
Less ostentatious, and yet studded thick
With hopeful gems. The rest, no portion left
That may disgrace his art, or disappoint
Large expectation, he disposes neat
At measur'd distances, that air and sun,
Admitted freely, may afford their aid,
And ventilate and warm the swelling buds.
Hence summer has her riches, autumn hence,
And hence ev'n winter fills his wither'd hand
With blushing fruits, and plenty, not his own.

PRUNING IN MARCH

Malapert March is parent to all these,
The sowing-time, when warmth begins to creep
Into the soil, as he who handles earth
With his bare hand well knows, and, stooping, feels
The sun on his bare nape, and as he kneels
On pad of sacking knows the stir of birth
Even as woman quickened stirs from sleep
And knows before all others in the deep
Instinct's communion that so much reveals,
The rite of the immediate future; so
Does the good gardener sense propitious time
And sows when seeds may grow
In the warm soil that follows on the rime
And on the breaking frost and on the snow.

And then in safety shall he prune
The rose with slicing knife above the bud
Slanting and clean; and soon
See the small vigour of the canted shoots
Strike outwards in their search for light and air,
Lifted above the dung about their roots,
Lifted above the mud.
Yet, unlike fashion's votary, beware
Of pruning so that but the stumps remain,
Miserly inches for the little gain

164

Of larger flower, exhibition's boast.
Neglect may hold a beauty of her own;
Neglected gardens in these years of war
When the fond owner wandered as a ghost
Only in thought, and longed to cut and trim
Having a vision of his roses prim
As they should be, what time the month was flown,
– Such gardens and their roses over-grown
As never in their careful life before
Flung to the daylight and the scented dark
With no man there to mark
A free and splendid tossing in a host
As unexpected as it had been rare.

THE WORK OF GARDENING

So manifold, all pleasing in their kind,
All healthful, are th' employs of rural life,
Reiterated as the wheel of time
Runs round; still ending, and beginning still.
Nor are these all. To deck the shapely knoll,
That, softly swell'd and gaily dress'd, appears
A flow'ry island, from the dark green lawn
Emerging, must be deem'd a labour due
To no mean hand, and asks the touch of taste.
Here also grateful mixture of well-match'd
And sorted hues (each giving each relief,
And by contrasted beauty shining more)
Is needful. Strength may wield the pond'rous spade,
May turn the clod, and wheel the compost home;
But elegance, chief grace the garden shows,
And most attractive, is the fair result
Of thought, the creature of a polish'd mind.
Without it all is gothic as the scene
To which th' insipid citizen resorts
Near yonder heath, where industry mispent,
But proud of his uncouth ill-chosen task,
Has made a heav'n on earth; with suns and moons
Of close-ramm'd stones has charg'd th' encumber'd soil,
And fairly laid the zodiac in the dust.
He, therefore, who would see his flow'rs dispos'd

Sightly and in just order, ere he gives
The beds the trusted treasure of their seeds,
Forecasts the future whole; that, when the scene
Shall break into its preconceiv'd display,
Each for itself, and all as with one voice
Conspiring, may attest his bright design.
Nor even then, dismissing as perform'd
His pleasant work, may he suppose it done.
Few self-supported flow'rs endure the wind
Uninjur'd, but expect th' upholding aid
Of the smooth-shaven prop, and, neatly tied,
Are wedded thus, like beauty to old age,
For int'rest sake, the living to the dead.
Some clothe the soil that feeds them, far diffus'd
And lowly creeping, modest and yet fair,
Like virtue, thriving most where little seen:
Some, more aspiring, catch the neighbour shrub
With clasping tendrils, and invest his branch,
Else unadorn'd, with many a gay festoon
And fragrant chaplet, recompensing well
The strength they borrow with the grace they lend.
All hate the rank society of weeds,
Noisome, and ever greedy to exhaust
Th' impov'rish'd earth; an overbearing race,
That, like the multitude made faction-mad,
Disturb good order, and degrade true worth.

WILLIAM COWPER   167

GARDENS OF THE WILD

If I could put my woods in song,
And tell what's there enjoyed,
All men would to my gardens throng,
And leave the cities void.

In my plot no tulips blow, –
Snow-loving pines and oaks instead;
And rank the savage maples grow
From spring's faint flush to autumn red.

My garden is a forest ledge
Which older forests bound;
The banks slope down to the blue lake-edge,
Then plunge to depths profound.

RALPH WALDO EMERSON
FROM "MY GARDEN"

THE WILD

Rich in her weeping Country's Spoils *Versailles*
May boast a thousand Fountains, that can cast
The tortured Waters to the distant Heav'ns;
Yet let me choose some Pine-topt Precipice
Abrupt and shaggy, whence a foamy Stream,
Like *Anio*, tumbling roars; or some bleak Heath,
Where straggling stand the mournful Juniper,
Or Yew-tree scath'd; while in clear Prospect round,
From the Grove's Bosom Spires emerge, and Smoak
In bluish Wreaths ascends, ripe Harvests wave,
Herds low, and Straw-rooft Cotts appear, and Streams
Beneath the Sun-beams twinkle – The shrill Lark,
That wakes the Wood-man to his early Task,
Or love-sick *Philomel*, whose luscious Lays
Sooth lone Night-wanderers, the moaning Dove,
Pitied by listening Milkmaid, far excell
The deep mouth'd Viol, the Soul-lulling Lute,
And Battle-breathing Trumpet. Artful Sounds!
That please not like the Choristers of Air,
When first they hail th' Approach of laughing *May*.

CONSERVATION

Soon I foresee few acres for harrowing
Left once the rich men's villas have seized the land;
   Fishponds that outdo Lake Lucrinus
     Everywhere; bachelor plane-trees ousting

Vine-loving elms; thick myrtle-woods, violet-beds,
All kinds of rare blooms tickling the sense of smell,
   Perfumes to drown those olive orchards
     Nursed in the past for a farmer's profit;

Quaint garden-screens, too, woven of laurel-boughs
To parry sunstroke. Romulus never urged
   This style of life; rough-bearded Cato
     Would have detested the modern fashions.

Small private wealth, large communal property –
So ran the rule then. No one had porticoes
   Laid out with ten-foot builder's measures,
     Catching the cool of the northern shadow,

No one in those days sneered at the turf by the
Roadside; yet laws bade citizens beautify
   Townships at all men's cost and quarry
     Glorious marble to roof the temples.

TRANSLATED BY JAMES MICHIE

PROSPECTS

And see the rivers how they run,
Thro' woods and meads, in shade and sun,
Sometimes swift, sometimes slow,
Wave succeeding wave, they go
A various journey to the deep,
Like human life to endless sleep!
Thus is nature's vesture wrought,
To instruct our wand'ring thought;
Thus she dresses green and gay,
To disperse our cares away.
Ever charming, ever new,
When will the landskip tire the view!
The fountain's fall, the river's flow,
The woody vallies, warm and low;
The windy summit, wild and high,
Roughly rushing on the sky!
The pleasant seat, the ruin'd tow'r,
The naked rock, the shady bow'r;
The town and village, dome and farm,
Each give each a double charm,
As pearls upon an Æthiop's arm.
See on the mountain's southern side,
Where the prospect opens wide,
Where the evening gilds the tide;
How close and small the hedges lie!

What streaks of meadows cross the eye!
A step methinks may pass the stream,
So little distant dangers seem;
So we mistake the future's face,
Ey'd thro' hope's deluding glass;
As yon summits soft and fair
Clad in colours of the air,
Which to those who journey near,
Barren, brown, and rough appear;
Still we tread the same coarse way,
The present's still a cloudy day.

AGAINST FORMAL GARDENS

    O how unlike the scene my fancy forms,
Did Folly, heretofore, with Wealth conspire
To plan that formal, dull, disjointed scene,
Which once was call'd a Garden. Britain still
Bears on her breast full many a hideous wound
Given by the cruel pair, when, borrowing aid
From geometric skill, they vainly strove
By line, by plummet, and unfeeling sheers,
To form with verdure what the builder form'd
With stone. Egregious madness; yet pursu'd
With pains unwearied, with expence unsumm'd,
And science doating. Hence the sidelong walls
Of shaven yew; the holly's prickly arms
Trimm'd into high arcades; the tonsile box
Wove, in mosaic mode of many a curl,
Around the figur'd carpet of the lawn.
Hence too deformities of harder cure:
The terras mound uplifted; the long line
Deep delv'd of flat canal; and all that toil,
Misled by tasteless Fashion, could atchieve
To mar fair Nature's lineaments divine.

WILLIAM MASON   175

THE GARDEN OF BERMUDA

Bermudas wall'd with Rocks, who does not know,
That happy Island, where huge Lemons grow,
And Orange trees which Golden Fruit do bear,
Th' Hesperian Garden boasts of none so fair?
Where shining Pearl, Coral, and many a pound,
On the rich Shore, of Amber-greece is found:
The lofty Cedar, which to Heaven aspires,
The Prince of Trees, is fewel for their Fires:
The smoak by which their loaded spits do turn,
For incense might, on Sacred Altars burn:
Their private Roofs on od'rous Timber born,
Such as might Palaces for Kings adorn.
The sweet *Palmettas* a new *Bacchus* yield,
With Leaves as ample as the broadest shield:
Under the shadow of whose friendly Boughs
They sit carowsing, where their Liquor grows.
Figs there unplanted through the Fields do grow,
Such as fierce *Cato* did the *Romans* show,
With the rare Fruit inviting them to spoil
Carthage the Mistriss of so rich a soil.
The naked Rocks are not unfruitful there,
But at some constant seasons every year,
Their barren tops with luscious Food abound,
And with the eggs of various Fowls are crown'd:
Tobacco is the worst of things, which they

To *English* Land-lords as their Tribute pay:
Such is the Mould, that the Blest Tenant feeds
On precious Fruits, and pays his Rent in Weeds:
With candid Plantines, and the jucy Pine,
On choicest Melons and sweet Grapes they dine;
And with Potatoes fat their wanton Swine.
Nature these Cates with such a lavish hand
Pours out among them, that our courser Land
Tastes of that bounty, and does Cloth return,
Which not for Warmth, but Ornament is worn:
For the king Spring which but salutes us here,
Inhabits there, and courts them all the year:
Ripe Fruits and blossoms on the same Trees live;
At once they promise, what at once they give:
So sweet the Air, so moderate the Clime;
None sickly lives, or dies before his time.
Heaven sure has kept this spot of earth uncurst,
To shew how all things were Created first . . .

EDMUND WALLER   177

THE MILL GARDEN

Stately stand the sunflowers, glowing down the
    garden-side,
Ranged in royal rank arow along the warm grey wall,
Whence their deep disks burn at rich midnoon afire
    with pride,
Even as though their beams indeed were sunbeams,
    and the tall
Sceptral stems bore stars whose reign endures, not
    flowers that fall.
Lowlier laughs and basks the kindlier flower of
    homelier fame,
Held by love the sweeter that it blooms in
    Shakespeare's name,
Fragrant yet as though his hand had touched and made
    it thrill,
Like the whole world's heart, with warm new life and
    gladdening flame.
Fair befall the fair green close that lies below the mill!

Softlier here the flower-soft feet of refluent seasons glide,
Lightlier breathes the long low note of change's
    gentler call.
Wind and storm and landslip feed the lone sea's gulf
    outside,

Half a seamew's first flight hence; but scarce may these
   appal
Peace, whose perfect seal is set for signet here on all.
Steep and deep and sterile, under fields no plough can
   tame,
Dip the cliffs full-fledged with poppies red as love or
   shame,
Wide wan daisies bleak and bold, or herbage harsh and
   chill;
Here the full clove pinks and wallflowers crown the
   love they claim.
Fair befall the fair green close that lies below the mill!

All the place breathes low, but not for fear lest ill betide,
Soft as roses answering roses, or a dove's recall.
Little heeds it how the seaward banks may stoop and
   slide,
How the winds and years may hold all outer things in
   thrall,
How their wrath may work on hoar church tower and
   boundary wall.
Far and wide the waste and ravin of their rule proclaim
Change alone the changeless lord of things, alone the
   same:
Here a flower is stronger than the winds that work
   their will,

Or the years that wing their way through darkness
    toward their aim.
Fair befall the fair green close that lies below the mill!

Friend, the home that smiled us welcome hither when
    we came,
When we pass again with summer, surely should reclaim
Somewhat given of heart's thanksgiving more than
    words fulfil –
More than song, were song more sweet than all but
    love, might frame.
Fair befall the fair green close that lies below the mill!

IN MY GARDEN

In my garden three ways meet,
Thrice the spot is blest;
Hermit thrush comes there to build
Carrier doves to rest.

The broad armed oaks, the copse's maze
The cold sea-wind detain;
And sultry summer overstays
When autumn chills the plain.

Self-sown my stately garden grows,
The winds and wind-blown seed,
Cold April rain, and colder snows
My hedges plant and feed.

From mountains far and valleys near,
The harvests sown to-day,
Thrive in all weathers without fear, –
Wild planters plant away!

In cities high the careful crowd
Of woe-worn mortals darkling go,
But in these sunny solitudes
My quiet roses blow.

Methought the sky looked scornful down
On all was base in man,
And airy tongues did taunt the town,
Achieve our peace who can!

What need I holier dew
Than Walden's haunted wave,
Distilled from heaven's alembic blue,
Steeped in each forest cave . . .

CITY GARDENS

See, in these roads, scarce conscious of a field,
What uniform varieties they yield! ...
Row smirks at row, each band-box has a brother
And half the causeway just reflects the other.
To beautify each close-wedged neighbour's door,
A strip of garden aims at length before;
Gritty in sunshine — yet, in showers, 'twill do,
Between a coach and house, to wet you through:
But soon, the public path, in envious sort,
Crosses, ... and cuts it at right angles, short.

GEORGE COLMAN, THE YOUNGER
FROM *LONDON RURALITY*

DE HORTIS JULII MARTIALIS

My Martial owns a garden, famed to please,
Beyond the glades of the Hesperides;
Along Janiculum lies the chosen block
Where the cool grottos trench the hanging rock.
The moderate summit, something plain and bare,
Tastes overhead of a serener air;
And while the clouds besiege the vales below,
Keeps the clear heaven and doth with sunshine glow.
To the June stars that circle in the skies
The dainty roofs of that tall villa rise.
Hence do the seven imperial hills appear;
And you may view the whole of Rome from here:
Beyond, the Alban and the Tuscan hills;
And the cool groves and the cool falling rills,
Rubre Fidenæ, and with virgin blood
Anointed once Perenna's orchard wood.
Thence the Flaminian, the Salarian way,
Stretch far broad below the dome of day;
And lo! the traveller toiling toward his home;
And all unheard, the chariot speeds to Rome!
For here no whisper of the wheels; and tho'
The Mulvian Bridge, above the Tiber's flow,
Hangs all in sight, and down the sacred stream
The sliding barges vanish like a dream,
The seaman's shrilling pipe not enters here,

Nor the rude cries of porters on the pier.
And if so rare the house, how rarer far
The welcome and the weal that therein are!
So free from access, the doors so widely thrown,
You half imagine all to be your own.

TRANSLATED BY R. L. STEVENSON

L'ALLÉE

As in the age of shepherd king and queen,
Painted and frail amid her nodding bows,
Under the sombre branches and between
The green and mossy garden-ways she goes,
With little mincing airs one keeps to pet
A darling and provoking perroquet.
Her long-trained robe is blue, the fan she holds
With fluent fingers girt with heavy rings,
So vaguely hints of vague erotic things
That her eye smiles, musing among its folds.
– Blonde too, a tiny nose, a rosy mouth,
Artful as that sly patch that makes more sly,
In her divine unconscious pride of youth,
The slightly simpering sparkle of the eye.

PAUL VERLAINE   187
TRANSLATED BY ARTHUR SYMONS

AN ATHENIAN GARDEN

The burned and dusty garden said:
"My leaves are echoes, and thy earth
Is packed with footsteps of the dead.

"The strength of spring-time brought to birth
Some needles on the crooked fir, –
A rose, a laurel – little worth.

"Come here, ye dreaming souls that err
Among the immortals of the grave:
My summer is your sepulchre.

"On earth what darker voices rave
Than now this sea-breeze, driving dust
And whirling radiance wave on wave,

"With lulls so fearful thro' the gust
That on the shapeless flower-bed
Like timber splits the yellow crust.

"O thirsty, thirsty are the dead,
Still thirsty, ever unallayed.
Where is no water, bring no bread."

I then had almost answer made,
When round the path in pleasure drew
Three golden children to the shade.

They stirred the dust with pail and hoe.
Then did the littlest from his fears
Come up and with his eyes of blue

Give me some berries seriously.
And as he turned to his brother, I
Looked after him thro' happy tears.

TRUMBULL STICKNEY

THE WIDOW'S LAMENT
IN SPRINGTIME

Sorrow is my own yard
where the new grass
flames as it has flamed
often before but not
with the cold fire
that closes round me this year.
Thirtyfive years
I lived with my husband.
The plumtree is white today
with masses of flowers.
Masses of flowers
load the cherry branches
and color some bushes
yellow and some red
but the grief in my heart
is stronger than they
for though they were my joy
formerly, today I notice them
and turn away forgetting.
Today my son told me
that in the meadows,

at the edge of the heavy woods
in the distance, he saw
trees of white flowers.
I feel that I would like
to go there
and fall into those flowers
and sink into the marsh near them.

THE ROOF GARDEN

A nervous hose is dribbling on the tar
This morning on this rooftop where I'm watching you
Move among your sparse, pinchpenny flowers,
Poor metronomes of color one month long
That pull the sun's rays in as best they can
And suck life up from one mere inch of dirt.
There's water in the sky but it won't come down.

Once we counted the skyline's water towers,
Barrels made of shingle, fat and high,
An African village suspended above
The needle hardness of New York that needs
More light than God provides to make it soft,
That needs the water in the water towers
To snake through pipe past all the elevators
To open up in bowls and baths and showers.

Soon our silence will dissolve in talk,
In talk that needs some water and some sun,
Or it will go the same way as before:
Dry repetitions of the ill we bear
Each other, the baited poles of light
Angling through the way the sun today
Fishes among the clouds.

Now you are through
Watering geraniums, and now you go
To the roof edge to survey the real estate
Of architectured air – tense forms wrought up,
Torn down, replaced, to be torn down again . . .
So much like us. Your head against the sky
Is topped by a tower clock, blocks away,
Whose two black hands are closing on the hour,
And I look down into the street below,
Rinsed fresh this morning by a water truck,
Down which a girl, perky in high heels,
Clops by, serenely unaware of us,
Of the cables, gas lines, telephone wires,
And water mains, writhing underfoot.

THE GARDEN AT ST. JOHN'S

Behind the wall of St. John's in the city
in the shade of the garden the Rector's wife
    walks with her baby a girl and the first
its mouth at her neck seeking and sucking
    in one hand holding its buttocks its skull
cupped by the other her arms like a basket
    of tenderest fruit and thinks as she fondles
the nape of the infant its sweat is like dew
    like dew and its hair is as soft as soft
as down as the down in the wingpits of angels

The little white dog with the harlequin eye
his tail like a thumb feet nimble as casters
    scoots in the paths of the garden's meander
behind the wall of St. John's in the city
    a toy deposed from his place in her arms
by this doll of the porcelain bone
    this pale living fruit without stone

She walks where the wrinkling tinkling fountain
    laps at the granite head of a monk
where dip the slippery noses of goldfish
    and tadpoles flip from his cuspid mouth
A miracle surely the young wife thinks
    from such a hard husband a tender child

and thinks of his black sleeves on the hymnbook
        inside the wall of St. John's in the city
the Ah of his stiff mouth intoning Amen
        while the organ prolongs its harmonious snore

Two trees like swans' necks twine in the garden
        beside the wall of St. John's in the city
Brooding and cool in the shade of the garden
        the scrolled beds of ivy glitter like vipers
A miracle surely this child and this garden
        of succulent green in the broil of the city
she thinks as setting the bird-cries apart
        she hears from beneath the dark spirals of ivy
under the wall of St. John's in the city
        the rectal rush and belch of the subway
roiling the corrugate bowels of the city
        and sees in the sky the surgical gleam
of an airplane stitching its way to the West
        above the wall of St. John's in the city
ripping its way through the denim air

THE GARDEN

High on his brick cliff his garden hung
Open eastward and backed against the
Heights that hid the broad, showy deathbed
Of the sun, whose Tiepolo gestures
He read raving reviews of in the
Fiery mirrors of the west-watching
Windows set in other distant cliffs.
It was there that he muttered about
His pots of spiky dill and broad mint,
His borders of concealing privet.
Edenist of the mid-air, he gazed
At the black oily kernels of dust
Flung as if by some high sower and
Languidly fallen through the forenoon
Over the walls, mingling with his soil.
He had had to make do among smut
And fruitless grit; had lopped and pruned all
The branches of shadow and with care
Hung the leathern mock-adder among
His greens to scare grumbling doves away.
In the evening cool his dull cigar
Breathed and glowed. This was all that there was
To keep. And there was nothing to lose.

GARDEN
(*Crete – New York*)

I

Petals fell white and remorseless as
snow layering sleep on sleep as sky
hands unrolled one endless bolt of dimity, and down
all floated, veiling the garden where
the real gardenia once, from its cumbrous vase,
exploded in a sand-grit gust to shed
benediction on the sleeping cat:
made the old woman laugh as it unloosed
dangerous sweetness on the air.

II

We lie, one closed corolla of winter limbs.
The room breathes drowsy with the scent of white
from the window plant. Dredged from sleep,
he yawns, stretches, prowls for clothes.

197

To return to the first gardenia:
in a sea-wind,
shattered.
In a Cretan garden, stars
of jasmine pitched straight down a wall.
Beyond drugged leaves, the rock
hoisted sheer up one hundred yards above
thistle and olive tangle to
caverned galleries where
the villagers – May, '41 – hid
from the shredded air, ten days.
That was the first invasion
conducted wholly from the sky.
The Germans stayed four years. The people took
to the rock.
But long ago, falling thick as centuries,
stone Turkish cannonballs had stunned
the land, and long
before that, the Mycenean spearheads drove
Minoans deep into their island's granite mind.

IV

The plant from Seventh Avenue
sits on the Ninth Street sill.
Leaves, at the florist's shining green,
cringe like small hands.
Aging, the flowers turn
mild butter yellow. But new buds twist
as pale green torches in the fists
of many liberties.
Light drawls in from the window,
delivers the room.
I rise from my sheets,
shake off my petals, veils of sleep,
water the potted gardenia from a jar.
It's morning. I begin.

I begin my life.

ROSANNA WARREN

PUBLIC GARDENS

Methinks I see the love that shall be made,
The Lovers walking in that amorous shade,
The Gallants dancing by the Rivers side,
They bathe in Summer, and in Winter slide,
Methinks I hear the Music in the Boats,
And the loud Echo which returns the Notes...

EDMUND WALLER, "ON ST. JAMES'S PARK,
AS LATELY IMPROV'D BY HIS MAJESTY"

LE JARDIN DES TUILERIES

This winter air is keen and cold,
　　And keen and cold this winter sun,
　　But round my chair the children run
Like little things of dancing gold.

Sometimes about the painted kiosk
　　The mimic soldiers strut and stride,
　　Sometimes the blue-eyed brigands hide
In the bleak tangles of the bosk.

And sometimes, while the old nurse cons
　　Her book, they steal across the square,
　　And launch their paper navies where
Huge Triton writhes in greenish bronze.

And now in mimic flight they flee,
　　And now they rush, a boisterous band –
　　And, tiny hand on tiny hand,
Climb up the black and leafless tree.

Ah! cruel tree! if I were you,
　　And children climbed me, for their sake
　　Though it be winter I would break
Into spring blossoms white and blue!

OSCAR WILDE　　　　　　　　　　　　　　　　　　203

LOTUS LAKE

By hand–drawn cart, an excursion at evening,
a carefree stroll in the Western Gardens.
Double conduits pour water into the lake,
rare trees line the streams that pass through,
their low limbs brushing my feathered carriage top,
their tall branches sweeping the azure sky.
A sudden wind lifts the carriage hubs,
flying birds start up before me.
The red of sunset flanks the bright moon,
gleaming stars come out between the clouds –
the heavens send down their shining colors,
their five hues fresh and clear!
Mine is not the long life of Sung or Ch'iao;
who can hope to be immortal like them?
With pleasures I will ease my heart,
take care to live out my hundred years!

        TRANSLATED BY BURTON WATSON

LINES WRITTEN IN
KENSINGTON GARDENS

In this lone, open glade I lie,
Screened by deep boughs on either hand;
And at its end, to stay the eye,
Those black-crowned, red-boled pine-trees stand!

Birds here make song, each bird has his,
Across the girdling city's hum.
How green under the boughs it is!
How thick the tremulous sheep-cries come!

Sometimes a child will cross the glade
To take his nurse his broken toy;
Sometimes a thrush flit overhead
Deep in her unknown day's employ.

Here at my feet what wonders pass,
What endless, active life is here!
What blowing daisies, fragrant grass!
An air-stirred forest, fresh and clear.

Scarce fresher is the mountain-sod
Where the tired angler lies, stretched out,
And, eased of basket and of rod,
Counts his day's spoil, the spotted trout.

In the huge world, which roars hard by,
Be others happy if they can!
But in my helpless cradle I
Was breathed on by the rural Pan.

I, on men's impious uproar hurled,
Think often, as I hear them rave,
That peace has left the upper world
And now keeps only in the grave.

Yet here is peace for ever new!
When I who watch them am away,
Still all things in this glade go through
The changes of their quiet day.

Then to their happy rest they pass!
The flowers upclose, the birds are fed,
The night comes down upon the grass,
The child sleeps warmly in his bed.

Calm soul of all things! make it mine
To feel, amid the city's jar,
That there abides a peace of thine,
Man did not make and cannot mar.

The will to neither strive nor cry,
The power to feel with others give!
Calm, calm me more! nor let me die
Before I have begun to live.

CASERTA GARDEN

Their garden has a silent tall stone-wall
So overburst with drowsing trees and vines,
None but a stranger would remark at all
The barrier within the fractured lines.

I doubt they know it's there, or what it's for –
To keep the sun-impasted road apart,
The beggar, soldier, renegade and whore,
The dust, the sweating ox, the screeching cart.

They'd say, "But this is how a garden's made":
To fall through days in silence dark and cool,
And hear the fountain falling in the shade
Tell changeless time upon the garden pool.

See from the tiptoe boy – the dolphin throats –
The fine spray bending; jets collapse in rings
Into the round pool, and each circle floats
Wide to the verge, and fails in shimmerings.

A childhood by this fountain wondering
Would leave impress of circle-mysteries:
One would have faith that the unjustest thing
Had geometric grace past what one sees.

How beauties will grow richer walled about!
This tortile trunk, old paradigm of pain,
These cherished flowers – they dream and look not out,
And seem to have no need of earth or rain.

In heavy peace, walled out necessity,
How devious the lavish grapevine crawls,
And trails its shade, irrelevant and free,
In delicate cedillas on the walls.

And still without, the dusty shouting way,
Hills lazar-skinned, with hungry-rooted trees,
And towns of men, below a staring day,
Go scattered to the turning mountain frieze.

The garden of the world, which no one sees,
Never had walls, is fugitive with lives;
Its shapes escape our simpler symmetries;
There is no resting where it rots and thrives.

RICHARD WILBUR   209

CENTRAL PARK

One November on a nervous amble
in the chilly dusk, we stop, turn, and fall.
The corresponding flurry of dry leaves
sweeps over us, spreadeagled as we are,
drenched in the early attitudes of lovers.
Leaves alone inhabit the charged space
between us, hint and crackle underneath,
behind, around, creeping into an ear
(dangerously), across the refusing
crook of arm and sluggish knee, against
brow and eyelid and the sweat, resting there.
Lips left bare for motion or meeting, we
will stir at the chosen moment and reach
for newer terrain under all these clothes.
When our backs arch and stiffen and shudder
we will shake off the ministering leaves,
and as if in agreement with each other
our bodies will mash the life out of them.

From THE PARKS

II

Gently gripped by the
avenues, left and right,
led by the beckoning
of some persistent wave,

you step all of a sudden
into the meeting place
of a shadowed water basin
and four stone benches;

in a separated time
that dwindles past alone.
On damp marble bases
where nothing any longer stands,

you raise a deep
expectant breath;
while the silver dripping
from the dark basin

already counts you among
its own and talks on.
And feeling yourself among stones
that listen, you don't stir.

VII

But there are bowls in which the Naiads'
reflections, no longer being bathed,
lie as if drowned, all twisted out of shape;
the avenues are closed by balustrades
in the distance as if barred.

A damp leaf-fall descends forever
through the air, as if on steps;
every bird's cry is as if notorious,
as if poisoned every nightingale.

Even spring is no longer lavish here,
these bushes don't believe in it;
grudgingly the gloomy, half-surviving
dried-up jasmine puts forth a stale fragrance

mingled with decay. As you walk along,
a swarm of gnats moves with you, as though
behind your back everything were being
instantly annihilated and erased.

TRANSLATED BY EDWARD SNOW

RUINED GARDENS

The lily's withered chalice falls
*   Around its rod of dusty gold,*
*   And from the beech-trees on the wold*
The last wood-pigeon coos and calls.

The gaudy leonine sunflower
*   Hangs black and barren on its stalk,*
*   And down the windy garden walk*
The dead leaves scatter, – hour by hour.

Pale privet-petals white as milk
*   Are blown into a snowy mass:*
*   The roses lie upon the grass*
Like little shreds of crimson silk.

OSCAR WILDE, "LE JARDIN"

From IN MEMORIAM

CI

Unwatched, the garden bough shall sway,
   The tender blossom flutter down,
   Unloved, that beech will gather brown,
This maple burn itself away;

Unloved, the sun-flower, shining fair,
   Ray round with flames her disk of seed,
   And many a rose-carnation feed
With summer spice the humming air;

Unloved, by many a sandy bar,
   The brook shall babble down the plain,
   At noon or when the lesser wain
Is twisting round the polar star;

Uncared for, gird the windy grove,
   And flood the haunts of hern and crake;
   Or into silver arrows break
The sailing moon in creek and cove;

Till from the garden and the wild
   A fresh association blow,
   And year by year the landscape grow
Familiar to the stranger's child;

As year by year the labourer tills
    His wonted glebe, or lops the glades;
    And year by year our memory fades
From all the circle of the hills.

THE GARDEN

There is a fenceless garden overgrown
With buds and blossoms and all sorts of leaves;
And once, among the roses and the sheaves,
The Gardener and I were there alone.

He led me to the plot where I had thrown
The fennel of my days on wasted ground,
And in that riot of sad weeds I found
The fruitage of a life that was my own.

My life! Ah, yes, there was my life, indeed!
And there were all the lives of humankind;
And they were like a book that I could read,
Whose every leaf, miraculously signed,
Outrolled itself from Thought's eternal seed.
Love-rooted in God's garden of the mind.

A FORSAKEN GARDEN

In a coign of the cliff between lowland and highland,
   At the sea-down's edge between windward and lee,
Walled round with rocks as an inland island,
   The ghost of a garden fronts the sea.
A girdle of brushwood and thorn encloses
   The steep square slope of the blossomless bed
Where the weeds that grew green from the graves
     of its roses
       Now lie dead.

The fields fall southward, abrupt and broken,
   To the low last edge of the long lone land.
If a step should sound or a word be spoken,
   Would a ghost not rise at the strange guest's hand?
So long have the gray bare walks lain guestless,
   Through branches and briers if a man make way,
He shall find no life but the sea-wind's, restless
      Night and day.

The dense hard passage is blind and stifled
    That crawls by a track none turn to climb
To the strait waste place that the years have rifled
    Of all but the thorns that are touched not of time.
The thorns he spares when the rose is taken;
    The rocks are left when he wastes the plain.
The wind that wanders, the weeds wind-shaken,
        These remain.

Not a flower to be prest of the foot that falls not;
    As the heart of a dead man the seed-plots are dry;
From the thicket of thorns whence the nightingale
        calls not,
    Could she call, there were never a rose to reply.
Over the meadows that blossom and wither
    Rings but the note of a sea-bird's song;
Only the sun and the rain come hither
        All year long.

The sun burns sere and the rain dishevels
    One gaunt bleak blossom of scentless breath.
Only the wind here hovers and revels
    In a round where life seems barren as death.
Here there was laughing of old, there was weeping,
    Haply, of lovers none ever will know,
Whose eyes went seaward a hundred sleeping Years ago.

Heart handfast in heart as they stood, "Look thither,"
    Did he whisper! "Look forth from the flowers to the sea;
For the foam-flowers endure when the rose-blossoms wither,
    And men that love lightly may die – but we?"
And the same wind sang and the same waves whitened,
    And or ever the garden's last petals were shed,
In the lips that had whispered, the eyes that had lightened,
        Love was dead.

Or they loved their life through, and then went whither?
    And were one to the end – but what end who knows?
Love deep as the sea as a rose must wither,
    As the rose-red seaweed that mocks the rose.
Shall the dead take thought for the dead to love them?
    What love was ever as deep as a grave?
They are loveless now as the grass above them
        Or the wave.

All are at one now, roses and lovers,
    Not known of the cliffs and the fields and the sea.
Not a breath of the time that has been hovers
    In the air now soft with a summer to be.
Not a breath shall there sweeten the seasons hereafter
    Of the flowers or the lovers that laugh now or weep,
When as they that are free now of weeping and laughter,
        We shall sleep.

Here death may deal not again forever;
    Here change may come not till all change end.
From the graves they have made they shall rise up never,
    Who have left nought living to ravage and rend.
Earth, stones, and thorns of the wild ground growing,
    While the sun and the rain live, these shall be;
Till a last wind's breath upon all these blowing
        Roll the sea.

Till the slow sea rise and the sheer cliff crumble,
    Till terrace and meadow the deep gulfs drink,
Till the strength of the waves of the high tides humble
    The fields that lessen, the rocks that shrink,
Here now in his triumph where all things falter,
    Stretched out on the spoils that his own hand spread,
As a god self-slain on his own strange altar,
        Death lies dead.

THE RAVAGED VILLA

In shards the sylvan vases lie,
　　Their links of dance undone,
And brambles wither by thy brim,
　　Choked fountain of the sun!
The spider in the laurel spins,
　　The weed exiles the flower:
And, flung to kiln, Apollo's bust
　　Makes lime for Mammon's tower.

IN AN ABANDONED GARDEN

My house is at the foot of the green cliff,
My garden, a jumble of weeds I no longer bother to mow.
New vines dangle in twisted strands
Over old rocks rising steep and high.
Monkeys make off with the mountain fruits,
The white heron crams his bill with fish from the pond,
While I, with a book or two of the immortals,
Read under the trees – mumble, mumble.

HAN-SHAN

TRANSLATED BY BURTON WATSON

TO A BOWER

Three times, sweet hawthorn, I have met thy bower,
    And thou hast gain'd my love, and I do feel
An aching pain to leave thee: every flower
    Around thee opening doth new charms reveal,
And binds my fondness stronger. – Wild wood bower,
    In memory's calendar thou'rt treasur'd up:
And should we meet in some remoter hour,
    When all thy bloom to winter-winds shall droop,
Ah, in life's winter, many a day to come,
    Should my grey wrinkles pass thy spot of ground,
And find it bare – with thee no longer crown'd,
    Within the woodman's faggot torn from hence,
Or chopt by hedgers up for yonder fence,
    Ah, should I chance by thee as then to come,
I'll look upon thy nakedness with pain,
    And, as I view thy desolated doom,
In fancy's eye I'll fetch thy shade again,
    And of this lovely day I'll think and sigh,
And ponder o'er this sweetly-passing hour,
    And feel as then the throes of joys gone by,
When I was young, and thou a blooming bower.

From THE DESERTED GARDEN

I mind me in the days departed,
How often underneath the sun
With childish bounds I used to run
   To a garden long deserted.

The beds and walks were vanished quite;
And wheresoe'er had struck the spade,
The greenest grasses Nature laid
   To sanctify her right.

I called the place my wilderness,
For no one entered there but I;
The sheep looked in, the grass to espy,
   And passed it ne'ertheless.

The trees were interwoven wild,
And spread their boughs enough about
To keep both sheep and shepherd out,
   But not a happy child.

Adventurous joy it was for me!
I crept beneath the boughs, and found
A circle smooth of mossy ground
   Beneath a poplar tree.

Old garden rose-trees hedged it in,
Bedropt with roses waxen-white
Well satisfied with dew and light
  And careless to be seen.

Long years ago it might befall,
When all the garden flowers were trim,
The grave old gardener prided him
  On these the most of all.

Some lady, stately overmuch,
Here moving with a silken noise,
Has blushed beside them at the voice
  That likened her to such.

And these, to make a diadem,
She often may have plucked and twined,
Half-smiling as it came to mind
  That few would look at *them*.

Oh, little thought that lady proud,
A child would watch her fair white rose,
When buried lay her whiter brows,
  And silk was changed for shroud!

Nor thought that gardener, (full of scorns
For men unlearned and simple phrase,)
A child would bring it all its praise
    By creeping through the thorns!

To me upon my low moss seat,
Though never a dream the roses sent
Of science or love's compliment,
    I ween they smelt as sweet.

It did not move my grief to see
The trace of human step departed:
Because the garden was deserted,
    The blither place for me! . . .

THE GARDEN SEAT

Its former green is blue and thin,
And its once firm legs sink in and in;
Soon it will break down unaware,
Soon it will break down unaware.

At night when reddest flowers are black
Those who once sat thereon come back;
Quite a row of them sitting there,
Quite a row of them sitting there.

With them the seat does not break down,
Nor winter freeze them, nor floods drown,
For they are as light as upper air,
They are as light as upper air!

A GARDEN OF GARDENS

If thou sitte here to viewe this pleasant garden place
Think thus: at last will come a frost, & all these floures deface:
But if thou sitte at ease to rest thy wearie bones,
Remember death brings finall rest to all oure greevous grones.
So whether for delight, or here thou sitte for ease,
Thinke still upon the latter day, so shalt thou God best please.

GEORGE GASCOIGNE
"ON A CHAYRE IN THE SAME GARDEN"

WHAT IS A GARDEN

All day working happily down near the stream bed
    the light passing into the remote opalescence
it returns to as the year wakes toward winter
    a season of rain in a year already rich
in rain with masked light emerging on all sides
    in the new leaves of the palms quietly waving
time of mud and slipping and of overhearing
    the water under the sloped ground going on
        whispering
as it travels time of rain thundering at night
    and of rocks rolling and echoing in the torrent
and of looking up after noon through the high branches
    to see fine rain drifting across the sunlight
over the valley that was abused and at last left
    to fill with thickets of rampant aliens
that brought habits but no stories under the mango trees
    already vast as clouds there I keep discovering
beneath the tangle the ancient shaping of water
    to which the light of an hour comes back as to a secret
and there I planted young palms in places I had not
        pondered
    until then I imagined their roots setting out in the dark
knowing without knowledge I kept trying to see them
        standing
    in that bend of the valley in the light that would come

THIS IS THE GARDEN

this is the garden: colours come and go,
frail azures fluttering from night's outer wing
strong silent greens serenely lingering,
absolute lights like baths of golden snow.
This is the garden: pursed lips do blow
upon cool flutes within wide glooms, and sing
(of harps celestial to the quivering string)
invisible faces hauntingly and slow.

This is the garden. Time shall surely reap
and on Death's blade lie many a flower curled,
in other lands where other songs be sung;
yet stand They here enraptured, as among
the slow deep trees perpetual of sleep
some silver-fingered fountain steals the world.

THE WORLD AS GARDEN

The figure of this world I can compare,
To Garden plots, and such like pleasaunt places,
The world breedes men of sundry shape and share,
As hearbes in gardens, grow of sundry graces:
Some good, some bad, some amiable faces,
Some foule, some gentle, some of froward mind,
Subject like bloome, to blast of every wind.

    And as you see the floures most fresh of hew,
That they prove not alwayes the holesomest,
So fayrest men are not alwayes found true:
But even as withred weedes fall from the rest,
So flatterers fall naked from their neast:
When truth hath tried, their painting tising tale,
They loose their glosse, and all their jests seeme stale.

    Yet some do present pleasure most esteeme,
Till beames of braverie wither all their welth,
And some agayne there be can rightly deeme,
Those herbes for best, which may mainteine their helth.
Considering well, that age drawes on by stelth,
And when the fayrest floure is shronke and gone,
A well growne roote, will stand and shifte for one.

    Then thus the restlesse life which men here leade,
May be resembled to the tender plant,
In spring it sprouts, as babes in cradle breede,
Florish in May, like youthes that wisdome want,

In Autumne ripes and rootes, least store waxe skante
In winter shrinks and shrowdes from every blast,
Like crooked age when lusty youth is past.
   And as the grounde or grace whereon it grewe,
Was fatte or leane, even so by it appeares,
If barreyn soyle, why then it chaungeth hewe,
It fadeth faste, it flits to fumbling yeares,
But if he gathered roote amongst his feeres,
And light on lande that was well muckte in deede,
Then standes it still, or leaves increase of seede.
   As for the reste, fall sundrie wayes (God wot)
Some faynt lyke froathe at every little puffe,
Some smarte by swoorde, like hearbes that serve the pot,
And some be weeded from the finer stuffe,
Some stande by proppes to maynteyne all their ruffe:
And thus (under correction bee it tolde)
Hath *Gascoigne* gathered in his Garden molde.

DOMICILIUM

It faces west, and round the back and sides
High beeches, bending, hang a veil of boughs,
And sweep against the roof. Wild honeysucks
Climb on the walls, and seem to sprout a wish
(If we may fancy wish of trees and plants)
To overtop the apple-trees hard by.

Red roses, lilacs, variegated box
Are there in plenty, and such hardy flowers
As flourish best untrained. Adjoining these
Are herbs and esculents; and farther still
A field; then cottages with trees, and last
The distant hills and sky.

Behind, the scene is wilder. Heath and furze
Are everything that seems to grow and thrive
Upon the uneven ground. A stunted thorn
Stands here and there, indeed; and from a pit
An oak uprises, springing from a seed
Dropped by some bird a hundred years ago.

                    In days bygone –
Long gone – my father's mother, who is now
Blest with the blest, would take me out to walk.
At such a time I once inquired of her
How looked the spot when first she settled here.
The answer I remember. "Fifty years
Have passed since then, my child, and change has
        marked
The face of all things. Yonder garden-plots
And orchards were uncultivated slopes
O'ergrown with bramble bushes, furze and thorn:
That road a narrow path shut in by ferns,
Which, almost trees, obscured the passer-by.

"Our house stood quite alone, and those tall firs
And beeches were not planted. Snakes and efts
Swarmed in the summer days, and nightly bats
Would fly about our bedrooms. Heathcroppers
Lived on the hills, and were our only friends;
So wild it was when first we settled here."

SUBURBAN GARDEN

Not wholly in the busy world, nor quite
Beyond it, blooms the garden that I love.
News from the humming city comes to it
In sound of funeral or of marriage bells;
And, sitting muffled in dark leaves, you hear
The windy clanging of the minster clock;
Although between it and the garden lies
A league of grass, washed by a slow broad stream,
That, stirred with languid pulses of the oar,
Waves all its lazy lilies, and creeps on,
Barge-laden, to three arches of a bridge
Crowned with the minster-towers.
                             The fields between
Are dewy-fresh, browsed by deep-uddered kine,
And all about the large lime feathers low,
The lime a summer home of murmurous wings.

TREES IN THE GARDEN

Ah in the thunder air
how still the trees are!

And the lime-tree, lovely and tall, every leaf silent
hardly looses even a last breath of perfume.

And the ghostly, creamy coloured little tree of leaves
white, ivory white among the rambling greens,
how evanescent, variegated elder, she hesitates on the
     green grass
as if, in another moment, she would disappear
with all her grace of foam!

And the larch that is only a column, it goes up too tall
     to see:
and the balsam-pines that are blue with the grey-blue
     blueness of things from the sea,
and the young copper beech, its leaves red-rosy at the
     ends
how still they are together, they stand so still
in the thunder air, all strangers to one another
as the green grass glows upwards, strangers in the
     garden.

A GARDEN BY THE SEA

I know a little garden-close,
Set thick with lily and red rose,
Where I would wander if I might
From dewy dawn to dewy night,
And have one with me wandering.

And though within it no birds sing,
And though no pillared house is there,
And though the apple-boughs are bare
Of fruit and blossom, would to God
Her feet upon the green grass trod,
And I beheld them as before.

There comes a murmur from the shore,
And in the place two fair streams are,
Drawn from the purple hills afar,
Drawn down unto the restless sea:
Dark hills whose heath-bloom feeds no bee,
Dark shore no ship has ever seen,
Tormented by the billows green
Whose murmur comes unceasingly
Unto the place for which I cry.

For which I cry both day and night,
For which I let slip all delight,
Whereby I grow both deaf and blind,
Careless to win, unskilled to find,
And quick to lose what all men seek.
Yet tottering as I am and weak,
Still have I left a little breath
To seek within the jaws of death
An entrance to that happy place,
To seek the unforgotten face,
Once seen, once kissed, once reft from me
Anigh the murmuring of the sea.

THE WEEPING GARDEN

The garden is frightful! It drips, it listens:
    Is the rain in loneliness here,
Squeezing a branch like lace at a window,
    Or is there a witness near?

The earth is heavy with swollen burdens;
    Smothered, the spongy weald.
Listen! Afar, as though it were August,
    Night ripens in a field.

No sound. Not a stranger around to spy
    The night. In the garden alone,
Rain starts up again, dripping and tumbling
    On roof, gutter, flagstone.

I'll bring the rain to my lips, and listen:
    Am I in loneliness here,
In the rain, bursting with tears, in darkness,
    Or is there a witness near?

Deep silence. Not even a leaf is astir.
    No gleam of light to be seen.
Only choking sobs and the splash of his slippers,
    And his sighs and tears between.

BORIS PASTERNAK   241
TRANSLATED BY EUGENE M. KAYDEN

THE GARDEN (*AFTER COWLEY*)

Fain would my muse the flow'ry treasures sing,
And humble glories of the youthful spring;
Where opening roses breathing sweets diffuse,
And soft carnations show'r their balmy dews;
Where lilies smile in virgin robes of white,
The thin undress of superficial light,
And vary'd tulips show so dazzling gay,
Blushing in bright diversities of day.
Each painted flouret in the lake below
Surveys its beauties, whence its beauties grow;
And pale Narcissus on the bank, in vain
Transformed, gazes on himself again.
Here aged trees cathedral walks compose,
And mount the hill in venerable rows:
There the green infants in their beds are laid,
The garden's hope, and its expected shade.
Here orange-trees with blooms and pendants shine,
And vernal honours to their autumn join;
Exceed their promise in the ripened store,
Yet in the rising blossom promise more.
There in bright drops the crystal fountains play,
By laurels shielded from the piercing day:
Where Daphne, now a tree as once a maid,
Still from Apollo vindicates her shade,
Still turns her beauties from th' invading beam,

242

Nor seeks in vain for succour to the stream.
The stream at once preserves her virgin leaves,
At once a shelter from her boughs receives,
Where summer's beauty midst of winter stays,
And winter's coolness spite of summer's rays.

HER GARDEN

Not at the full moon will she pick those flowers
For sudden shade indoors would make them wilt.
The petals would drop down on polished wood
Adding another element to decay
Which all her old rooms are infected with.

Only outside she can put off the course
Of her disease. She has the garden built
Within high walls so no one can intrude.
When people pass she only hears the way
Their footsteps sound, never their closer breath.

But in her borders she observes the powers
Of bud and branch, forgetting how she felt
When, blood within her veins like sap, she stood,
Her arms like branches bare above the day
And all the petals strewn along her path.

No matter now for she has bridged the pause
Between fruition and decay. She'll halt
A little in her garden while a mood
Of peace so fills her that she cannot say
Whether it is the flowers' life or her death.

AND THEN...

Bad-tempered, I got back:
Then, in the garden,
The willow-tree.

ŌSHIMA RYŌTA
TRANSLATED BY GEOFFREY BOWNAS
AND ANTHONY THWAITE

ACKNOWLEDGMENTS

Thanks are due to the following copyright holders for permission to reprint:

CAMPANA, DINO: 'Autumn Garden', from *Sappho to Valery*, translated by J.F. Nims. Copyright © 1990 the University of Arkansas Press. Reprinted by permission of the University of Arkansas Press. CRANE, HART: 'Garden Abstract', from *Complete Poems of Hart Crane*, edited by Marc Simon. Copyright 1933, © 1958, 1966 by Liveright Publishing Corporation. Copyright © 1986 by Marc Simon. Reprinted by permission of Liveright Publishing Corporation. CUMMINGS, E.E.: 'this is the garden: colours come and go', is reprinted from *Complete Poems 1904–1962* by E.E. Cummings, edited by George J. Firmage, by permission of W.W. Norton & Company Ltd. Copyright © 1925, 1976, 1991 by the Trustees for the E.E. Cummings Trust. DAVIE, DONALD: 'Gardens no Emblems', from *Collected Poems*. Reprinted by permission of Carcanet Press. DE LA MARE, WALTER: 'Myself', from *The Complete Poems of Walter de la Mare*, 1969. Reprinted by permission of The Literary Trustees of Walter de la Mare, and The Society of Authors as their representative. EMERSON, RALPH WALDO: 'My Garden' and 'In my garden'. By permission of the Ralph Waldo Emerson Memorial Association. EZRA, IBN: 'The Garden of Song', from *The Jewish Poets of Spain*, Penguin Books Ltd., translated by David Goldstein. Reprinted by permission of David Higham Associates. FROST, ROBERT: 'A Girl's Garden', from *The Poetry of Robert Frost*, edited by Edward Connery Lathem. Reprinted by permission of Jonathan Cape Ltd. GRAVES, ROBERT: 'Gardener', from *Collected Poems* (Vol I) (US: *Collected Poems: 1975*. Copyright © 1975 by Robert Graves).

246

INDEX OF AUTHORS

ANONYMOUS: The Seeds of Love   62

MATTHEW ARNOLD (1822–88):
 Lines Written in Kensington Gardens 205

THE BIBLE *From* Genesis   17

 From The Song of Solomon   45

WILLIAM BLAKE (1757–1827): The Garden of Love   59

NICOLAS BOILEAU (1636–1711):
 The Garden of Writing   90

ROBERT BRIDGES (1844–1930):
 The Garden in September 106

ELIZABETH BARRETT BROWNING (1806–61):
 From The Deserted Garden 225

ROBERT BROWNING (1812–89): The Flower's Name 127

DINO CAMPANA (1885–1932): Autumn Garden 109

THOMAS CAMPION (d. 1619): Cherry Ripe   49

GEOFFREY CHAUCER (1345?–1400): Love's Garden   47

JOHN CLARE (1793–1864): To a Bower 224

L. J. M. (Lucius Junius Moderatus) COLUMELLA
 (1ST CENTURY AD): Autumnal Work 161

GEORGE COLMAN, THE YOUNGER (1762–1836):
 From London Rurality 183

WILLIAM COWPER (1721–1800): On Pruning 163

 The Work of Gardening 166

HART CRANE (1899–1932): Garden Abstract   61

E. E. CUMMINGS (1894–1962): This is the garden .. 232

ERASMUS DARWIN (1731–1802): The Poppy 121
AUSTIN DOBSON (1840–1921):
    From A Garden Song 95
DONALD DAVIE (1922–95): Gardens no Emblems .. 143
WALTER DE LA MARE (1873–1956): Myself 88
JOHN DONNE (1572–1631): Twicknam Garden 56
JOHN DYER (1700–58): Prospects 173
RALPH WALDO EMERSON (1803–82):
    From My Garden 169
    In my garden 181
ROBERT FROST (1874–1963): A Winter Eden 112
    A Girl's Garden 146
GEORGE GASCOIGNE (1525?–77):
    Inscription in a Garden 15
    On a Chayre in the same Garden 229
    The World as Garden 233
ROBERT GRAVES (1895–1985): Gardener 139
DEBORA GREGER (1949–): The Garden 44
NICHOLAS GRIMALD (1519–62): The Garden 32
THOM GUNN (1929–): The Garden of the Gods .. 34
HAFIZ (d. *c.* 1390): The Lesson of the Flowers 118
HAN YÜ (768–824): Flowering Plums 117
HAN-SHAN (fl. 627–649): In an Abandoned Garden 223
THOMAS HARDY (1840–1928): The Garden Seat .. 228
    Domicilium 235
ANTHONY HECHT (1923–):
    La Condition Botanique 38

HEINRICH HEINE (1797–1856):

On a radiant summer morning 115

GEORGE HERBERT (1593–1633): Paradise 25

ROBERT HERRICK (1591–1674): To a Bed of Tulips 122

HUGO VON HOFMANNSTHAL (1874–1929):

The Emperor of China Speaks 149

JOHN HOLLANDER (1929–): The Garden 196

MARTHA HOLLANDER (1959–): Central Park 210

HOMER (8TH CENTURY BC?):

The Gardens of Alcinous 23

HORACE (65–8 BC): Conservation 172

WILLIAM DEAN HOWELLS (1837–1920): November .. 110

MOSES IBN EZRA (c. 1066– c. 1139):

The Garden of Song 73

JALĀL AL-DĪN RŪMI (1207–73):

What the Flowers Said 131

ELIZABETH JENNINGS (1926–): Her Garden 244

JOHN KEATS (1795–1821): A Garden-Dream 85

WALTER SAVAGE LANDOR (1775–1864):

The Gardener 154

D. H. LAWRENCE (1885–1930): Trees in the Garden 238

JAY MACPHERSON (1931–):

The Garden of the Sexes 60

A Garden Shut 81

KATHERINE MANSFIELD (1888–1923):

Out in the garden 137

MARTIAL (AD 40–103/4): De Hortis Julii Martialis 185

252

ANDREW MARVELL (1621–78): The Garden   76
    The Mower Against Gardens 159
WILLIAM MASON (1725–97):
    Against Formal Gardens 175
J. D. McCLATCHY (1945–): Weeds 130
HERMAN MELVILLE (1819–91): The Ravaged Villa .. 222
GEORGE MEREDITH (1828–1909):
    The Garden of Epicurus   89
JAMES MERRILL (1926–95): A Vision of the Garden   75
W. S. MERWIN (1927–): What is a garden   231
EDNA ST. VINCENT MILLAY (1892–1950):
    The Hardy Garden   71
    Spring in the Garden   97
JOHN MILTON (1608–74): Eden   19
    From Paradise Lost 155
WILLIAM MORRIS (1834–96):
    Thunder in the Garden 100
    A Garden by the Sea 239
HOWARD MOSS (1922–87): The Roof Garden 192
ŌSHIMA RYŌTA (1718–87): And then 245
OVID (43 BC–AD 17):
    Before Gardens: The Golden Age   21
BORIS PASTERNAK (1890–1960):
    The Weeping Garden 241
OCTAVIO PAZ (1914–): A Doomed Garden   83
ANGELO POLIZIANO (1454–94):
    She Finds Herself in a Garden   50

253

JOHN POMFRET (1667–1702): No Barren Leaves .. 92
ALEXANDER POPE (1688–1744):

    To build, to plant.... 156

    The Garden 242

THOMAS RANDOLPH (1605–35): On Grafting 158

RENÉ RAPIN (1621–87): Of Roses and Hyacinths .. 120

ADRIENNE RICH (1929–): Design in Living Colors 69

RAINER MARIA RILKE (1875–1926): *From* The Parks 211

EDWIN ARLINGTON ROBINSON (1869–1935):

    The Garden 217

THEODORE ROETHKE (1908–63): Transplanting 157

ISAAC ROSENBERG (1890–1918): The Garden of Joy 36

CHRISTINA ROSSETTI (1830–94):

    An October Garden 108

DANTE GABRIEL ROSSETTI (1828–82): Silent Noon .. 58

SABA (fl. early 19TH CENTURY):

    A King's Garden World 26

V. (VITA) SACKVILLE-WEST (1892–1962): Frost 111

    The Rose 124

    Pruning in March 164

SAIGYŌ (1118–90): In Winter 114

WILLIAM SHAKESPEARE (1564–1616):

    The Gardener's Lesson 144

JAMES SHIRLEY (1596–1666): The Garden 79

EDMUND SPENSER (1552?–99): In the Bower of Bliss 52

    The Garden of Adonis 54

WALLACE STEVENS (1879–1955): Banal Sojourn 103

254

ROBERT LOUIS STEVENSON (1850–94): The Gardener   142

TRUMBULL STICKNEY (1874–1904):

An Athenian Garden   188

MAY SWENSON (1913–89): The Garden at St. John's   194

ALGERNON CHARLES SWINBURNE (1837–1909):

The Garden of Proserpine   65

The Mill Garden   178

A Forsaken Garden   218

ALFRED, LORD TENNYSON (1850–92):

An Arabian Night Garden   29

Song   113

Come into the garden, Maud   133

From In Memoriam   215

Suburban Garden   237

EDWARD THOMAS (1878–1917): Digging   151

JAMES THOMSON (1700–48): Late Spring   98

TS'AO P'I (187–266): Lotus Lake   204

MARK VAN DOREN (1894–1972): Gardener   140

MONA VAN DUYN (1921–):

The Gardener to His God   152

PAUL VERLAINE (1844–96): L'Allée   187

EDMUND WALLER (1606–87):

The Garden of Bermuda   176

From On St. James's Park, as Lately Improv'd

by His Majesty   201

ROBERT PENN WARREN (1905–89): The Garden   104

ROSANNA WARREN (1953–): Garden   197

JOSEPH WARTON (1722–1800): The Wild 171
RICHARD WILBUR (1921–): Caserta Garden 208
OSCAR WILDE (1854–1900):
    Le Jardin des Tuileries 203
    Le Jardin 213
WILLIAM CARLOS WILLIAMS (1883–1963):
    The Tulip Bed 123
    The Widow's Lament in Springtime 190
YVOR WINTERS (1900–68): Time and the Garden .. 87

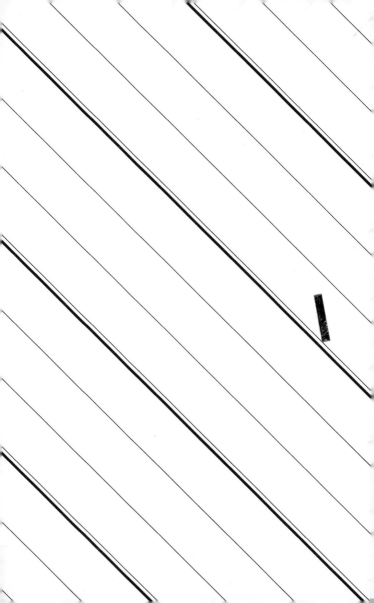